DIABETIC AIR FRYER COOKBOOK

300 DIABETIC-FRIENDLY RECIPES TO LIVE A HEALTHY AND ENERGETIC LIFE WITHOUT GIVING UP YOUR FAVORITE AIR FRIED MEALS.
INCLUDES A 30-DAY MEAL PLAN

Aileen Terry

Table of Contents

Introduction

Diabetes is a disease with many names, but for this book's purposes, the term diabetes will mean diabetes mellitus. The word diabetes means "sugar," which refers to a disease characterized by high blood sugar. Diabetes is usually diagnosed by finding out that a patient's blood sugar is higher than normal. There are two main types of diabetes — type 1 and type 2. Type 1 diabetes is an autoimmune disease, so your body's immune system turns on itself. In this form of diabetes, your body stops making insulin, a hormone that helps your body absorb the sugar in food to produce energy. Type 1 is lifelong and always requires treatment.

Type 2 diabetes is an illness where either the body no longer has enough insulin or can't use it effectively. A primary cause of type 2, which can affect adults and children, is obesity, which causes the body to lose its ability to use insulin properly. If you have type 2 diabetes, you must take proper care of yourself to prevent complications such as damage to the eyes, heart, blood vessels, or kidney failure. Diabetes control can prevent these complications.

The Diabetes Air Fryer Cookbook was written as a guide for those who are new to the world of air fryers and want to learn what they can do with them. It takes information from a variety of sites and eBooks. We hope you find this book helpful in understanding your new air fryer and how you can make great meals in it!

Are you a diabetic who loves to cook? If so, you know that you have to take special care when preparing your meals. But your air fryer can make cooking easier and healthier for you. This is because your air fryer can cook your food without oil or grease. This is great for people on a low-fat diet or just trying to eat fwer fat-laden foods. But it also makes using your air fryer easier and safer for those with diabetes.

The number of options and benefits offered by your air fryer is astounding. With this device, you can cook a wide range of foods that previously may have been forbidden because of high fat or sugar levels. With an air fryer, you can prepare ready-to-eat meals that are healthy and nutritious for you. They also take less time to prepare than traditional oven or stovetop cooking methods, making them perfect for busy people like students, commuters, and shift workers.

The benefits extend beyond healthier food, though — they can help you lose weight and cut down on your "bad" cholesterol and triglycerides levels! This makes using your air fryer both healthier and more cost-effective than other cooking methods.

Chapter 1. What is Diabetes?

Diabetes is a well-being condition that occurs when the body's blood glucose is high. Glucose is a source of energy for your body. Think of your body as a car that needs gasoline as fuel to help it move. Insulin, a hormone made in the pancreas, transports glucose from the bloodstream to the cells where it will be used as energy.

When your body doesn't make enough insulin, doesn't make insulin, or can't use the insulin made the proper way, you will develop diabetes. This will cause a buildup in the blood, stopping glucose from getting into cells for energy.

Types of Diabetes

Type 1 Diabetes

A deficiency of the immune system results in Type 1 diabetes, also called insulin-dependent diabetes or juvenile diabetes. In the pancreas, your immune system destroys the insulin-producing cells, killing the body's capacity to create insulin. It's not clear what causes autoimmune disease and how to treat it effectively. Take insulin to survive with Type 1 diabetes. As an infant or young adult, several individuals are diagnosed. The body will show on the onset of type 1 diabetes polyuria (excessive excretion of urine), polydipsia (extreme thirst), sudden weight loss, and constant hunger, fatigue, and vision changes. These changes can occur suddenly.

Type 2 Diabetes

Type 2 diabetes, formerly denoted as adult-onset diabetes or non-insulin-dependent, stems from insufficient insulin utilization by the body. Type 2 diabetes is found in most individuals with diabetes. The symptoms can be identical to those with type 1 diabetes. However, much less marked, as a result, the condition can be detected after many years of diagnosis when symptoms have already occurred.

Type 2 diabetes happens when sugar adds up in your blood, and the body becomes resistant to insulin. Type 2 diabetes is insulin resistance, which ultimately leads to obesity; obesity is a collection of different diseases. Older generations were more susceptible, but more and younger generations are now being affected. This is a product of poor health, not enough nutrition, and fitness patterns. Your pancreas avoids using insulin properly in type 2 diabetes. This creates complications with sugar that has to be taken out of the blood and placing it for energy in the cells. Finally, this will add to the need for insulin treatment.

Earlier stages, such as prediabetic, can be controlled successfully through food, exercise, and dynamic blood sugar control. This will also avoid the overall progression of type 2 diabetes. It is possible to monitor diabetes. If sufficient adjustments to the diet are created, the body will receive remission.

Gestational Diabetes

Hyperglycemia with blood glucose levels above average, but below those diabetes levels is diagnosed with gestational diabetes. Gestational diabetes is identified via prenatal tests rather than by signs recorded — high blood sugar, which also occurs during gestation. Hormones produced by the placenta are insulin-blocking, which is the major cause of this type of diabetes. You can manage gestational diabetes most of the time by food and exercise. Usually, it gets resolved after delivery. During pregnancy, gestational diabetes will raise the risk of complications. It will also increase the likelihood that both mothers and infants may experience type 2 diabetes later in life. Insulin-blocking hormones shaped by the placenta cause this type of diabetes.

Causes of Diabetes

Your cells can become immune to insulin's effect in prediabetic, which can happen in type 2 diabetes, and the pancreas cannot generate sufficient insulin to counteract this resistance. Sugar builds up in your bloodstream instead of going to your cells, where it's required for fuel. It is unclear why this arises, while hereditary and environmental influences are thought to play a role in the progress of type 2 diabetes. The advancement of type 2 diabetes is closely related to being overweight, although not everybody with type 2 is obese. Several variables, including dietary conditions and genetic makeup, handle the most prevalent type of diabetes.

Here are a few factors:

Insulin Resistance

Type 2 diabetes commonly progresses with insulin resistance, a disease in which insulin is not handled well by the body, liver, and fat cells. To enable glucose to reach cells, the body requires more insulin. The pancreas initially generates more insulin to maintain the additional demand. The pancreas cannot create enough insulin over time, and blood glucose levels increase.

Overweight, Physical Inactivity, and Obesity

When you are not regularly active and are obese or overweight, you are much more prone to have type 2 diabetes. Often, excess weight induces insulin resistance, prominent in persons with type 2 diabetes. In which area of the body stores fat counts a lot. Insulin tolerance, type 2 diabetes, and heart and blood artery dysfunction are attributed to excess belly fat.

Genes and Family History

A family history of diabetes makes it more probable that gestational diabetes may occur in a mother, which means that genes play a part. In African Americans, Asians, American Indians, and Latinas, Hispanic, mutations can also justify why the disease happens more frequently.

Any genes can make you more susceptible to advance type 2 diabetes to type 1 diabetes.

Genetic makeup can make a person more obese, which in turn leads to having type 2 diabetes.

Signs of Having a Diabetes

Many of the same unmistakable warning signals are present with all forms of diabetes.

Itchy skin and Dry mouth: Since the body requires water to urinate, most items provide less moisture. You can get dehydrated, and that might make your mouth taste dry. And dehydration also makes skin dry, which makes you itchy.

Tiredness and Hunger: Your body transforms the food you consume into (sugar) glucose that body cells use for fuel. But insulin is required by your cells to take in glucose. And if the body does not produce enough or none of the insulin or the insulin body produces is immune to your cells, the glucose can't get into them, and you don't have energy. This will leave you hungrier than normal and more drained.

Urinating and Getting Thirstier: Peeing and getting thirstier most frequently. Typically, the average person needs to pee 4 to 7 times in one day, although developing diabetes may go a lot faster because normally, when it moves into your liver, your body reabsorbs glucose. But as diabetes drives your blood sugar up, it may not be practical for your kidneys to get it all back down. This allows more urine to be created by the liver, and it requires fluids. The outcome: you're going to have to urinate more frequently. You will get thirsty when you urinate too much. Hence drinking more water.

Blurred Vision: As your body cannot process fluids more efficiently, which leads to the swelling of lenses in your eyes. Hence, they have changed shape and cannot focus as before. It results in blurred vision.

Hence, to prevent the onset of diabetes, it is important to eat healthily, stay active, eat less junk food, and monitor your blood glucose levels regularly.

Obesity and Diabetes

Diabetes is a stubborn condition that arises from 2 causes: when the pancreas cannot produce insulin enough for body needs or whenever the body's insulin may not be used properly. Insulin is a blood sugar-regulating hormone. Hyperglycemia, or high blood sugar, is a typical result of uncontrolled diabetes, causing significant harm to the body's structures, especially blood vessels and nerves. Diabetes mellitus is a category of illness that influences how the body uses glucose. Glucose is essential to your well-being. The cells that create muscles and tissues require a significant glucose supply. It's the brain's primary power supply, too. The primary issue of diabetes varies based on the type of diabetes. And this can cause excessive sugar in the blood, no matter what diabetes a person has. If there is too much sugar, it can lead to grave health issues. The insulin hormone transfers the sugar into the cells from the blood.

High blood sugar levels may cause harm to your kidneys, eyes, organs, and nerves.

To understand the major reason for diabetes, you should know the body's normal glucose consumption route.

How to Prevent?

Type 1 Diabetes cannot currently be prevented; no preventive strategy has proven effective. However, preventive action for conditions like Type 2 Diabetes which are believed to help prevent Type 1 Diabetes includes these:

- Prefer foods low in fat and calories; consume fruit and vegetables in abundance.
- Engage in moderate aerobic physical activity for at least 20 to 30 minutes per day (or 150 minutes per week).
- Keeping a fit weight, avoiding conditions like overweight and obesity.

Chapter 2. What Is Air Frying?

An air fryer is comparable to an oven in how it roasts and bakes. Still, the distinction is that the heating elements are situated only on top and supported by a strong, large fan, which results in very crisp food in no time. The air fryer uses spinning-heated air to easily and uniformly cook food instead of using a pot of hot oil. To encourage the hot air to flow evenly around the meal, the meal is put in a metal basket (mesh) or a rack, producing the same light golden, crispy crunch you get from frying in oil. It is easy to use air fryers. Besides, they cook food faster than frying and clean up quickly. You can prepare a selection of healthy foods such as fruits, beef, seafood, poultry, and more, besides making beneficial variants of your favorite fried foods such as chips, onion rings, or French fries.

The air fryer is the modern kitchen tool that is proving its worth in effectively reducing the risk of diabetes, weight loss, and living a healthier life without compromising on fried, fatty, and high-calorie food.

How it Works

The air fryer is a convective heat oven with a revved-up countertop. Its small room enables cooking much quicker. A heating device and a fan are kept at the top of the device. Hot air flows through and around food put in a basket-type fryer. This fast circulation, just like deep frying, renders the food crisp. It's also super quick to clean up, and most systems include dishwasher-safe components.

Tips for Cooking

Shake the Basket: open the fryer and move food around while cooking in the device's tray, squeezing smaller foods such as French fries and chips. Toss them every 5–10 minutes for better performance.

Do not overcrowd the Basket: Giving plenty of room to foods so that the air will efficiently circulate is what gets you crispy outcomes.

Spray oil on the Food: Make sure the food doesn't cling to the bowl; gently brush foods with cooking spray.

Keep the Food Dry: To prevent splattering and excessive smoke, make sure food is dry before frying (even if you marinate it). In the same way, be sure to remove the grease from the bottom of the machine regularly while preparing high-fat items such as chicken wings.

Know Other Functions of Air Frying: The air fryer is not just for frying, it is also perfect for other healthier cooking methods, such as grilling, baking, and roasting.

Few other tips are:

- Cut the food into equally sized parts for uniform cooking.
- Distribute the food in one thin, even layer in the air fryer basket. If you crowded the basket, food can be less crispy.
- A tiny amount of oil would create the same light, golden, crispy crust from frying. I use cooking spray or an oil mister to apply a thin, even oil coating to the food.
- The air fryer is useful for reheating foods, particularly with a crispy crust that you want.

Benefits of Air Fryer with Diabetes

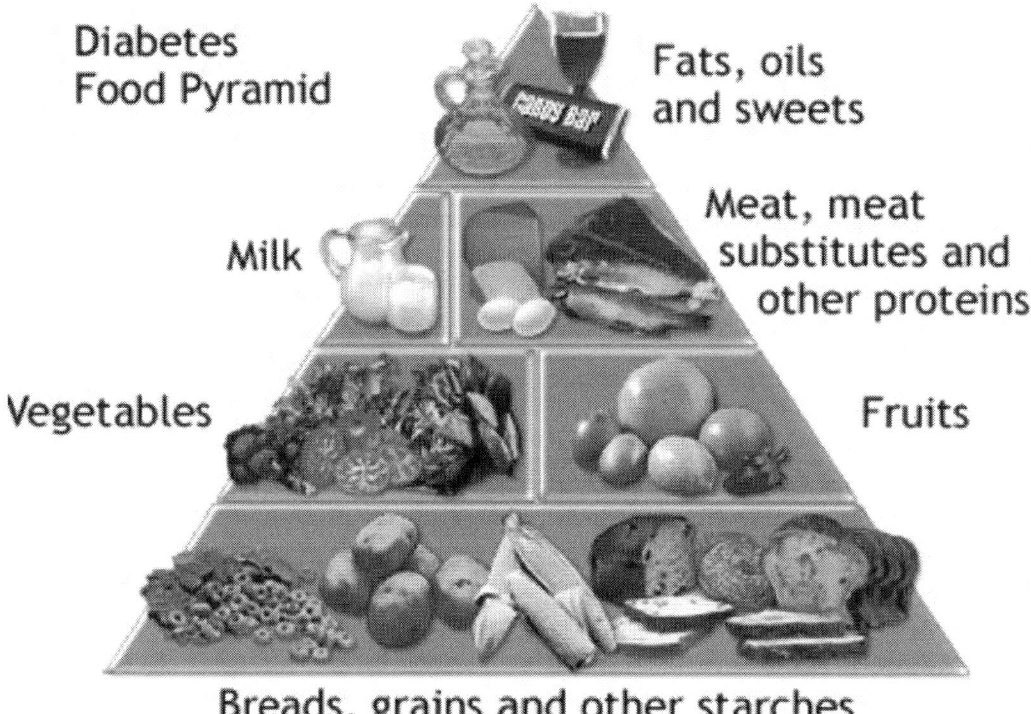

According to this food pyramid, you must consume a large portion of healthy vegetables and whole-grain starches, a balanced amount of healthy fats, and proteins with small amounts of nuts and oils.

Benefits:

- Easy cleanup
- Low-fat meals
- Less oil is needed
- Hot air cooks food evenly
- Weight loss
- Reduced cancer risk
- Diabetes management
- Improved memory
- Improved gut health

Chapter 3. Breakfast Recipes

1. Almond Pancakes

Preparation time: 10 minutes
Cooking time: 4 minutes
Servings: 6
Ingredients:

- 1 ½ cups almond flour
- 1 tsp. baking soda
- ½ tsp. apple cider vinegar
- 1 tsp. vanilla extract
- 1 Tbsp. ground cinnamon
- 1 Tbsp. Erythritol
- 1 Tbsp. coconut butter, softened
- 1 cup almond milk
- Cooking spray

Directions:

1. In a mixing bowl, make the pancake batter: combine almond flour, baking soda, apple cider vinegar, vanilla extract, ground cinnamon, coconut butter, and almond milk.
2. Whisk the mixture until smooth and homogenous. Then spray the insides of 6 ramekins with cooking spray
3. Fill ½ of every ramekin with pancake batter and top with Erythritol.
4. Arrange the ramekins in the air fryer basket and close the lid.
5. Cook the pancakes for 4 minutes at 395°F.
6. The pancakes are cooked when they have a light brown surface.

Nutrition:
Calories 167
Fat 2.3
Fiber 1.4
Carbs 31.1
Protein 4.6

2. Eggs and Peppers

Preparation time: 10 minutes
Cooking time: 10 minutes
Servings: 2
Ingredients:

- 2 tsps. coconut butter
- ¼ tsp. ground black pepper
- ¾ tsp. ground turmeric
- 4 eggs, cracked
- 1 large bell pepper

Directions:

1. Cut the bell pepper into halves and remove the seeds.
2. Place the coconut butter inside each bell pepper half.
3. Add 2 cracked eggs in each bell pepper half and top them with ground black pepper and turmeric.
4. Arrange the pepper boats in the air fryer basket and close the lid.
5. Cook the peppers for 10 minutes at 365°F or until the eggs are firm.

Nutrition:
Calories 182
Fat 12.8
Fiber 1.1
Carbs 5.9
Protein 11.8

3. Sweet Toasts

Preparation time: 10 minutes
Cooking time: 6 minutes
Servings: 4
Ingredients:

- 4 whole-grain bread slices
- 2 eggs, beaten
- ¼ cup coconut milk
- 1 tsp. almond flour
- 1 tsp. ground cinnamon
- 1 Tbsp. Erythritol
- Cooking spray

Directions:

1. Whisk together beaten eggs and coconut milk.
2. Add almond flour and stir until smooth.
3. Dip the bread slices in the egg mixture and leave them for 5 minutes, or until the bread soaks up the milk mixture.
4. Meanwhile, preheat the air fryer to 375°F.
5. Spray the air fryer baking pan with cooking spray.
6. Place the dipped bread slices in the baking pan and insert them in the air fryer.
7. Close the lid and cook the toasts for 3 minutes.
8. Then flip them to the other side and cook for an additional 3 minutes.
9. The cooked toasts will have a golden-brown crust.
10. In a shallow bowl, mix together the Erythritol and cinnamon.
11. Sprinkle the cooked hot toasts with the cinnamon mixture on both sides.

Nutrition:
Calories 76
Fat 2.8
Fiber 0.5
Carbs 8.9
Protein 4

4. Chili Eggs

Preparation time: 10 minutes
Cooking time: 11 minutes
Servings: 2

Ingredients:

- 4 eggs
- ¾ tsp. salt
- ¾ tsp. chili flakes
- 1 cup ice water, for peeling

Directions:

1. Place the eggs in the air fryer basket and close the lid.
2. Cook the eggs for 11 minutes at 270°F.
3. When the eggs are cooked, place them in the ice water immediately and leave for 5 minutes.
4. Peel the eggs and cut them into halves.
5. Sprinkle each egg half with chili flakes and salt.

Nutrition:

Calories 126
Fat 8.8
Fiber 0
Carbs 0.7
Protein 11.1

5. Fruit Fritters

Preparation time: 10 minutes
Cooking time: 10 minutes
Servings: 4

Ingredients:

- 1 cup almond flour
- 2 apples, grated
- 1 egg, beaten
- 2 Tbsps. plain yogurt
- 1 Tbsp. Erythritol
- ½ tsp. vanilla extract
- 1 tsp. avocado oil

Directions:

1. Make the fritters dough: in a bowl combine almond flour, grated apples, egg, plain yogurt, Erythritol, and vanilla extract.
2. Mix the mixture with a spoon.
3. Line the bottom of the air fryer basket with parchment and brush it with avocado oil.
4. With a spoon make fritters and place them in the air fryer basket.
5. Close the lid and cook fritters for 10 minutes at 375°F.
6. Flip the fritters after 5 minutes of cooking.

Nutrition:

Calories 203
Fat 3.3
Fiber 6.4
Carbs 40.7
Protein 6

6. Cabbage Cakes

Preparation time: 15 minutes
Cooking time: 9 minutes
Servings: 6

Ingredients:

- 1 cup cabbage, shredded
- 1 egg, beaten
- 2 Tbsps. plain yogurt
- 1 tsp. salt
- ½ cup almond flour
- ¼ tsp. ground cumin
- 1 tsp. olive oil

Directions:

1. Mix together the shredded cabbage and salt.
2. Leave the shredded cabbage for 10 minutes or until it releases its water. Drain the excess liquid.
3. Then add egg, plain yogurt, flour, and ground cumin.
4. Mix the fritter mixture well.
5. Brush the air fryer baking pan with olive oil.
6. With a spoon make medium size fritters and place them in the baking pan.
7. Insert the baking pan in the preheated to the 385°F air fryer.
8. Close the lid and cook the fritters for 5 minutes.
9. Flip them and bake for 4 minutes more.

Nutrition:

Calories 62
Fat 1.7
Fiber 0.6
Carbs 9.1
Protein 2.5

7. Asparagus Salad

Preparation Time: 5 minutes
Cooking Time: 10 minutes
Servings: 4

Ingredients:

- 1 cup baby arugula
- 1 bunch asparagus, trimmed
- 1 Tbsp. balsamic vinegar
- 1 Tbsp. cheddar cheese, grated
- A pinch of salt and black pepper
- Cooking spray

Directions:

1. Put the asparagus in your air fryer's basket, grease with cooking spray, season with salt and pepper, and cook at 360°F for 10 minutes.
2. Take a bowl and mix the asparagus with the arugula and the vinegar, toss, divide between plates and serve hot with cheese sprinkled on top

Nutrition:

Calories: 200

Fat: 5g
Fiber: 1g
Carbs: 4g
Protein: 5g

8. Zucchini Squash Mix

Preparation Time: 10 minutes
Cooking Time: 35 minutes
Servings: 2

Ingredients:

- 1 lb. zucchini, sliced
- 1 Tbsp. parsley, chopped
- 1 yellow squash, halved, deseeded, and chopped
- 1 Tbsp. olive oil
- Pepper
- Salt

Directions:

1. Add all ingredients into the large bowl and mix well.
2. Transfer mixture into the air fryer basket and cook at 400°F for 35 minutes.
3. Serve and enjoy.

Nutrition:

Calories: 49
Fat: 3 g
Carbs: 4 g
Sugar: 2 g
Protein: 1.5 g

9. Bacon-Wrapped Filet Mignon

Preparation Time: 10 minutes
Cooking Time: 15 minutes
Servings: 2

Ingredients:

- 2 bacon slices
- 2 (4 ounce) filet mignon
- Salt and ground black pepper, as needed
- Olive oil cooking spray

Directions:

1. Wrap 1 bacon slice around each filet mignon and secure with toothpicks.
2. Lightly season the fillets with salt and black pepper.
3. Arrange the filet mignon onto a cooling rack and spray with cooking spray.
4. Arrange the drip pan in the bottom of the Air Fryer Oven cooking chamber.
5. Select "Air Fry" and then adjust the temperature to 375°F.
6. Set the timer for 15 minutes and press the "Start".
7. When the display shows "Add Food" insert the cooking rack in the center position.
8. When the display shows "Turn Food" turn the filets.
9. When cooking time is complete, remove the rack from Air fryer oven and serve hot.

Nutrition:

Calories: 360
Fat: 19.6 g
Carbs: 0.4 g
Protein: 42.6 g

10. Pumpkin Pancakes

Preparation Time: 15 minutes
Cooking Time: 12 minutes
Servings: 2

Ingredients:

- 1 square puff pastry
- 3 Tbsps. pumpkin filling
- 1 small egg, beaten

Directions:

1. Roll out a square of puff pastry and cut it into 8 equal-sized square pieces. Layer each square with pumpkin pie filling, leaving about ¼-inch space around the edges. Coat the edges with the beaten egg.
2. Press "Power Button" of Air Fry Oven and turn the dial to select the "Air Fry" mode. Press the Time button and again turn the dial to set the cooking time to 12 minutes. Now push the Temp button and rotate the dial to set the temperature at 355°F. Press the "Start/Pause" button to start. When the unit beeps to show that it is preheated, open the lid. Arrange the squares into a greased "Sheet Pan" and insert them in the oven. Bake until done. Serve warm.

Nutrition:

Calories: 109
Fat: 6.7 g
Carbs: 9.8 g
Fiber: 0.5 g
Sugar: 2.6 g
Protein: 2.4 g

11. Onion Omelet

Preparation Time: 10 minutes
Cooking Time: 15 minutes
Servings: 2

Ingredients:

- 4 eggs
- ¼ tsp. low-sodium soy sauce
- Ground black pepper, as needed
- 1 tsp. butter
- 1 medium yellow onion, sliced
- ¼ cup Cheddar cheese, grated

Directions:

1. In a skillet, melt the butter over medium heat and cook the onion for about 8-10 minutes.
2. Remove from the heat and set aside to cool slightly.
3. Meanwhile, in a bowl, add the eggs, soy sauce, and black pepper and beat well.
4. Add the cooked onion and gently stir to combine.
5. Place the onion mixture into a small baking pan. Press "Power Button" of Air Fry Oven and turn the dial to select the "Air Fry" mode.
6. Press the Time button and again turn the dial to set the cooking time to 5 minutes.
7. Now push the Temp button and rotate the dial to set the temperature at 355°F. Press the "Start/Pause" button to start.
8. When the unit beeps to show that it is preheated, open the lid.
9. Arrange pan over the "Wire Rack" and insert in the oven. Cook until done.
10. Cut the omelet into 2 portions and serve hot.

Nutrition:
Calories: 222
Fat: 15.4 g
Fat: 6.9 g
Carbs: 6.1 g
Fiber: 1.2 g
Sugar: 3.1 g
Protein: 15.3 g

12. Blackberries Bowls

Preparation Time: 20 minutes
Cooking Time: 10 minutes
Servings: 4
Ingredients:

- 1 ½ cups coconut milk
- ½ cup coconut, shredded
- ½ cup blackberries
- 2 tsp. stevia

Directions:

1. In your air fryer's pan, mix all the ingredients, stir, cover and cook at 360°F for 15 minutes.
2. Divide into bowls and serve

Nutrition:
Calories: 171
Fat: 4g
Fiber: 2g
Carbs: 3g
Protein: 5g

13. Breakfast Pockets

Preparation Time: 15 minutes
Cooking Time: 30 minutes
Servings: 4
Ingredients:

- 2 sheets (17.25 oz.) almond flour puff pastry, cut into 4 equal sized pieces
- 1 package (6 oz.) ground breakfast sausage, crumbled
- 2 eggs, lightly beaten
- 1 cup cheddar cheese, shredded
- 1 tsp. kosher salt
- ½ tsp. ground black pepper
- 2 Tbsps. canola oil

Directions:

1. Preheat the Air fryer to 375°F and grease the Air fryer basket.
2. Arrange the sausage in the basket and roast for about 15 minutes.
3. Place the eggs into the basket and cook for about 5 minutes.
4. Season with salt and black pepper and divide the egg sausages mixture over the 4 puff pastry rectangles.
5. Top with shredded cheddar cheese and drizzle with canola oil.
6. Place 1 egg pocket in the basket and cook for 6 minutes at 400°F.
7. Remove from the Air fryer and repeat with the remaining pockets.
8. Serve warm and enjoy.

Nutrition:
Calories: 197
Fats: 15.4g
Carbs: 8.5g
Sugar: 1.1g
Proteins: 7.9g
Sodium: 203mg

14. Ham and Egg Toast Cups

Preparation Time: 5 minutes
Cooking Time: 5 minutes
Servings: 2
Ingredients:

- 2 eggs
- 2 slices of ham
- 2 Tbsps. butter
- Cheddar cheese, for topping
- Salt, to taste
- Black pepper, to taste

Directions:

1. Preheat the Air fryer to 400°F and grease 2 ramekins with melted butter.

2. Place each ham slice in the greased ramekins and crack each egg over ham slices.
3. Sprinkle with salt, black pepper and cheddar cheese and transfer into the Air fryer basket.
4. Cook for about 5 minutes and remove the ramekins from the basket.

Serve warm.

Nutrition:

Calories: 202
Fat: 13.7g
Carbs: 7.4g
Sugar: 3.3g
Protein: 10.2g
Sodium: 203mg

15. Cauliflower Hash Brown

Preparation Time: 20 minutes
Cooking Time: 10 minutes
Servings: 4

Ingredients:

- 2 cups cauliflower, finely grated, soaked and drained
- 2 Tbsps. xanthan gum
- Salt, to taste
- Ground pepper, to taste
- 2 tsps. chili flakes
- 1 tsp. garlic
- 1 tsp. onion powder
- 2 tsps. vegetable oil

Directions:

1. Preheat the Air fryer to 300°F and grease an Air fryer basket with oil.
2. Heat vegetable oil in a nonstick pan and add cauliflower.
3. Sauté for about 4 minutes and dish out the cauliflower in a baking dish.
4. Mix the cauliflower with xanthum gum, salt, chili flakes, and garlic and onion powder.
5. Mix well and refrigerate the hash for about 20 minutes.
6. Place the hash in the Air fryer basket and cook for about 10 minutes.
7. Flip the hash after cooking half way through and dish out to serve warm.
8. **Nutrition:**

Calories: 291
Fat: 2.8g
Carbs: 6.5g
Sugar: 4.5g
Protein: 6.6g
Sodium: 62mg

16. French Toast Sticks

Preparation Time: 10 minutes
Cooking Time: 5 minutes
Servings: 4

Ingredients:

- 4 slices bread, cut into sticks
- 2 Tbsps. soft butter or margarine
- 2 eggs, beaten
- Salt, to taste
- 1 pinch cinnamon
- 1 pinch nutmeg
- 1 pinch ground cloves

Directions:

1. Preheat the Air fryer at 365°F and grease an Air fryer pan with butter.
2. Whisk eggs with salt, cinnamon, nutmeg and ground cloves in a bowl.
3. Dip the bread sticks in the egg mixture and place in the pan.
4. Cook for about 5 minutes, flipping halfway, and remove from the Air fryer when done.
5. Dish out and serve warm.

Nutrition:

Calories: 186
Fat: 11.7g
Carbs: 6.8g
Sugar: 1.7g
Protein: 13.2g
Sodium: 498mg

17. Sausage Solo

Preparation Time: 5 minutes
Cooking Time: 22 minutes
Servings: 4

Ingredients:

- 6 eggs
- 4 cooked sausages, sliced
- 2 slices bread, cut into sticks
- ½ cup mozzarella cheese, grated
- ½ cup cream

Directions:

1. Preheat the Air fryer to 355°F and grease 4 ramekins lightly.
2. Whisk together eggs and cream in a bowl and beat well.
3. Transfer the egg mixture into ramekins and arrange the bread sticks and sausage slices around the edges.
4. Top with mozzarella cheese and place the ramekins in Air fryer basket.
5. Cook for about 22 minutes and dish out to serve warm.

Nutrition:
Calories: 180,
Fat: 12.7g,
Carbs: 3.9g,
Sugar: 1.3g,
Protein: 12.4g,
Sodium: 251mg

18. Sausage Bacon Fandango

Preparation Time: 5 minutes
Cooking Time: 20 minutes
Servings: 4
Ingredients:

- 8 bacon slices
- 8 chicken sausages
- 4 eggs
- Salt and black pepper, to taste

Directions:

1. Preheat the Air fryer to 320°F and grease 4 ramekins lightly.
2. Place bacon slices and sausages in the Air fryer basket.
3. Cook for about 10 minutes and crack 1 egg in each prepared ramekin.
4. Season with salt and black pepper and cook for about 10 more minutes.
5. Divide bacon slices and sausages on serving plates.
6. Place 1 egg in each plate and serve warm.

Nutrition:
Calories: 287
Fat: 21.5g
Carbs: 0.9g
Sugar: 0.3g
Protein: 21.4g
Sodium: 1007mg

19. Creamy Parsley Soufflé

Preparation Time: 5 minutes
Cooking Time: 10 minutes
Servings: 2
Ingredients:

- 2 eggs
- 1 Tbsp. fresh parsley, chopped
- 1 fresh red chili pepper, chopped
- 2 Tbsps. light cream
- Salt, to taste

Directions:

1. Preheat the Air fryer to 390°F and grease 2 soufflé dishes.
2. Mix together all the ingredients in a bowl until well combined.
3. Transfer the mixture into prepared soufflé dishes and place in the Air fryer.
4. Cook for about 10 minutes and dish out to serve warm.

Nutrition:
Calories: 108
Fat: 9g
Carbs: 1.1g
Sugar: 0.5g
Protein: 6g
Sodium: 146mg

20. Breakfast Zucchini & Cream Muffins

Preparation Time: 5 minutes
Cooking Time: 15 minutes
Servings: 5
Ingredients:

- 1 Tbsp. cream cheese
- Half a cup zucchini, shredded
- 1 Tbsp. plain yogurt
- 1 egg
- 1 cup milk
- 2 Tbsps. warmed coconut oil
- Pinch of sea salt
- 2 tsps. baking powder
- 1 tsp. cinnamon
- 1 Tbsp. liquid Stevia
- 4 cups whole wheat flour

Directions:

1. Mix all your dry ingredients in a mixing bowl (flour, sea salt, baking powder and cinnamon). Stir to combine.
2. In another mixing bowl combine all of the wet ingredients (coconut oil, milk, yogurt, liquid Stevia, and egg). Whisk these until evenly combined.
3. In a large bowl combine both the wet and dry ingredients and use a hand mixer to whisk them. Stir in the shredded zucchini and fold in the cream cheese.
4. Place five muffin cups into your air fryer. Fill each cup ¾ full of mixture. Set air fryer to 350°F and cook muffins for 12 minutes. Serve warm or cold.

Nutrition:
Calories: 217
Total Fat: 9.3g
Carbs: 8g
Protein: 10.2g

21. Hard-Boiled Eggs

Preparation Time: 2 minutes
Cooking Time: 10 minutes
Servings: 6 eggs

Ingredients:

- 6 eggs

Directions:

1. Arrange raw eggs on the rack of your air fryer, leaving enough space between the eggs for the air to circulate.
2. Cook the eggs for fifteen minutes in the fryer at 260°F.
3. Remove the eggs from the fryer and submerge them in a bowl of ice-water for 10 minutes. Peel the eggs and serve.
4. Enjoy!

Nutrition:
Calories: 62
Fat: 4 g (1 g saturated fat)
Cholesterol: 163 mg
Sodium: 62 mg
Protein: 5 g.

22. Grilled Cheese Sandwiches

Preparation Time: 2 minutes
Cooking Time: 10 minutes
Servings: 2 sandwiches

Ingredients:

- 4 slices American cheese
- 4 slices whole-wheat sandwich bread
- Butter, as needed

Directions:

1. Warm your air fryer to 360°F.
2. Fill the center of 2 bread slices with two slices of American cheese.
3. Spread an even layer of butter on each side of the sandwich and position it in the basket of your air fryer in a single layer.
4. Air-fry the sandwiches for 4 minutes, flipping once, and cook for another 3 to 4 minutes until toasted.
5. Serve!

Nutrition:
Calories: 297
Fat: 14.6 g (7.5 g saturated fat)
Cholesterol: 39 mg
Sodium: 832 mg
Carbohydrates: 31.3 g
Dietary Fiber: 1 g
Total sugars: 7.1 g
Protein: 11.8 g

23. Hot Dogs

Preparation Time: 2 minutes
Cooking Time: 10 minutes
Servings: 4

Ingredients:

- 4 beef hot dogs

Directions:

1. Using a knife, score the hot dogs to create several little slits to prevent bursting during cooking.
2. Lay the hotdogs in the air fryer.
3. Bake for 5 minutes at 375°F.
4. When the timer is up, rotate the hotdogs; cook for 3 minutes longer.
5. Remove from fryer and dig in.
6. Serve!

Nutrition:
Calories: 111
Fat: 6 g (2 g saturated fat)
Cholesterol: 20 mg
Sodium: 307 mg
Carbohydrates: 8 g
Protein: 4 g

24. Perfect Cinnamon Toast

Preparation Time: 2 minutes
Cooking Time: 20 minutes
Servings: 12 slices

Ingredients:

- 1 stick butter at room temperature
- 1 ½ tsp. vanilla extract
- 1 ½ tsp. ground cinnamon
- ½ cup Splenda
- 1 pinch kosher salt
- 2 pinches freshly ground black pepper
- 12 slices whole-wheat bread

Directions:

1. Using the back of your spoon, mash the butter until soft.
2. Add the Splenda, vanilla, salt, cinnamon and pepper, and stir to combine fully.
3. Spread about 1/12 of the butter mixture onto the bread, covering up to the edges.
4. Load 4 bread slices into the air fryer basket and cook for 5 minutes at 400°F. Repeat until all the bread has been toasted.
5. Remove toasted bread from the fryer.
6. Cut diagonally and serve while hot.
7. Enjoy!

Nutrition:
Calories: 355
Fat: 17 g (10 g saturated fat)
Cholesterol: 40 mg
Sodium: 432 mg
Carbohydrates: 45 g
Dietary Fiber: 3 g
Total Sugars: 5 g
Protein: 6 g

25. Mushroom and Cheese Frittata

Preparation Time: 20 minutes
Cooking Time: 20 minutes
Servings: 4

Ingredients:

- 6 eggs
- 6 cups button mushrooms, sliced thinly
- 1 red onion, sliced into thin rounds
- 6 Tbsp. Feta cheese, reduced fat, crumbled
- Pinch of salt
- 2 Tbsp. Olive oil

Directions:

1. Preheat Air Fryer to 330°F.
2. Sauté onions and mushrooms. Transfer to a plate with a paper towel.
3. Meanwhile, beat the eggs in a bowl.
4. Season with salt. Coat a baking dish with cooking spray. Add the egg mixture.
5. Add in mushrooms and onions. Top with crumbled feta cheese.
6. Place baking dish in the Air fryer basket. Cook for 20 minutes. Serve.

Nutrition:

Calorie: 140
Carbohydrate: 5.4 g
Fat: 10.6 g
Protein: 22.7 g
Fiber: 1.2 g

26. Cinnamon and Cheese Pancake

Preparation Time: 5–7 minutes
Cooking Time: 10 minutes
Servings: 4

Ingredients:

- 2 eggs
- 2 cups cream cheese, reduced-fat
- ½ tsp. cinnamon
- 1 pack Stevia

Directions:

1. Preheat Air Fryer to 330°F.
2. Meanwhile, combine cream cheese, cinnamon, eggs, and stevia in a mixer and beat until well combined.
3. Pour ¼ of the mixture in the air fryer basket. Cook for 2 minutes on each side. Repeat the process with the rest of the mix. Serve.

Nutrition:

Calorie: 140
Carbohydrate: 5.4 g
Fat: 10.6 g
Protein: 22.7 g
Fiber: 1.2 g

27. Low-Carb White Egg and Spinach Frittata

Preparation Time: 12-15 minutes
Cooking Time: 12 minutes
Servings: 4

Ingredients:

- 8 egg whites
- 2 cups fresh spinach
- 2 Tbsp. olive oil
- 1 green pepper, seeds removed and chopped
- 1 red pepper, seeds removed and chopped
- ½ cup feta cheese, reduced fat, crumbled
- ¼ yellow onion, chopped
- 1 tsp. salt
- 1 tsp. pepper

Directions:

1. Warm the Air Fryer to 330°F.
2. Meanwhile, place red and green peppers and onions in the Air Fryer basket, and cook for 3 minutes. Season with salt and pepper.
3. Pour egg whites over and cook for 4 minutes. Add the spinach and feta cheese on top.
4. Cook for 5 minutes.
5. Transfer to a plate, slice, and service.

Nutrition:

Calorie: 120
Carbohydrate: 13 g
Fat: 4.5 g
Protein: 9.9 g
Fiber: 1.2 g

28. Scallion Sandwich

Preparation Time: 10 minutes
Cooking Time: 10 minutes
Servings: 1

Ingredients:

- 2 slices wheat bread
- 2 tsp. butter, low fat
- 2 scallions, sliced thinly
- 1 Tbsp. parmesan cheese, grated
- ¾ cup cheddar cheese, reduced-fat, grated

Directions:

1. Preheat the Air fryer to 356°F.
2. Spread butter on a slice of bread. Place inside the cooking basket with the butter side facing down.
3. Place cheese and scallions on top. Spread the rest of the butter on the other slice of bread, put it on top of the sandwich, and sprinkle with parmesan cheese.
4. Cook for 10 minutes.

Nutrition:

Calorie: 154

Carbohydrate: 9 g
Fat: 2.5 g
Protein: 8.6 g
Fiber: 2.4 g

29. Air Fried Eggs

Preparation Time: 15 minutes
Cooking Time: 15 minutes
Servings: 4

Ingredients:

- 4 eggs
- 2 cups baby spinach, rinsed
- 1 Tbsp. extra-virgin olive oil
- ½ cup cheddar cheese, reduced-fat, shredded, divided
- 4 slices bacon
- Pinch salt
- Pinch pepper

Directions:

1. Preheat the Air Fryer to 350°F.
2. Warm oil in a pan over medium-high flame. Cook the spinach until wilted. Drain the excess liquid. Put the cooked spinach into four greased ramekins.
3. Add a slice of bacon to each ramekin, crack an egg in each ramekin, and put cheese on top.
4. Season with salt and pepper.
5. Put the ramekins inside the cooking basket of the Air Fryer.
6. Cook for 15 minutes.

Nutrition: facts:

Calorie: 106
Carbohydrate: 10 g
Fat: 3.2 g
Protein: 9.0 g
Fiber: 1.2 g

30. Cinnamon Pancake

Preparation Time: 15 minutes
Cooking Time: 10 minutes
Servings: 4

Ingredients:

- 2 eggs
- 2 cups low-fat cottage cheese
- ½ tsp. cinnamon
- 1 pack Stevia

Directions:

1. Preheat Air Fryer to 330°F.
2. Combine cottage cheese, cinnamon, eggs and stevia in a blender and pulse until well combined.
3. Pour ¼ of the mixture in the air fryer basket.
4. Cook for 2 minutes on each side.
5. Repeat the process with the rest of the mixture. Serve.

Nutrition:

Calorie: 106
Carbohydrate: 10 g
Fat: 3.2 g
Protein: 9.0 g
Fiber: 1.2 g

31. Spinach and Mushrooms Omelet

Preparation Time: 15 minutes
Cooking Time: 10 minutes
Servings: 4

Ingredients:

- ½ cup spinach leaves
- 1 cup sliced mushrooms
- 3 green onions, chopped
- 1 cup water
- ½ tsp. turmeric
- ½ red bell pepper, sliced
- 2 Tbsp. butter, low-fat
- 1 cup almond flour
- ½ tsp. onion powder
- ½ tsp. garlic powder
- ½ tsp. fresh ground black pepper
- ¼ tsp. ground thyme
- 2 Tbsps. extra-virgin olive oil
- 1 tsp. black salt
- Salsa, store-bought, to taste

Directions:

1. Preheat the Air Fryer to 300°F.
2. Rinse spinach leaves with water. Set aside.
3. In a mixing bowl, combine green onions, onion powder, garlic powder, turmeric, thyme, olive oil, and pepper. Mix well.
4. In another bowl, combine water and flour to form a smooth paste. Add in the spice mixture and mix well.
5. In a pan, heat olive oil. Sauté peppers and mushrooms for 3 minutes. Tip in spinach and cook for 3 minutes until spinach is wilted. Set aside.
6. Pour the omelet batter into the air fryer basket. Cook for 3 minutes before flipping. Cook for a further 3 minutes until done. Place vegetables on top. Season with salt.
7. Serve with salsa on the side.

Nutrition:

Calorie: 110
Carbohydrate: 9 g
Fat: 1.3 g
Protein: 5.4 g
Fiber: 1.0 g

32. All Berries Pancakes

Preparation Time: 15 minutes
Cooking Time: 10 minutes
Servings: 4

Ingredients:

- ½ cup frozen blueberries, thawed
- ½ cup frozen cranberries, thawed
- 1 cup coconut milk
- 2 Tbsp. coconut oil, for greasing
- 2 Tbsp. stevia
- 1 cup whole wheat flour, finely milled
- 1 Tbsp. baking powder
- 1 tsp. vanilla extract
- ¼ tsp. salt

Directions:

1. Preheat Air Fryer to 330°F.
2. In a mixing bowl, combine coconut oil, coconut milk, flour, stevia, baking powder, vanilla extract, and salt. Gently fold in berries.
3. Divide batter into equal portions. Spoon into the Air fryer basket. Flip once the edges are set. Do not press down on pancakes.
4. Transfer to a plate. Sprinkle with stevia. Serve.

Nutrition:
Calorie: 57
Carbohydrate: 14 g
Fat: 0.3 g
Protein: 0.7 g
Fiber: 2.4 g

33. Ham and Cheese English muffin Melt

Preparation Time: 10 minutes
Cooking Time: 3 minutes
Servings: 2

Ingredients:

- 1 whole-grain English muffin, split and toasted
- 2 tsps. Dijon mustard
- 2 slices tomato
- 4 thin slices deli ham
- ½ cup shredded Cheddar cheese
- 2 large eggs, fried (optional)

Directions:

1. Spread each toasted English muffin half with 1 tsp. of mustard and place them on a rimmed baking sheet, cut-side up.
2. Top each with a tomato slice and 2 slices of ham. Sprinkle each with half of the cheese.
3. Set the air fryer to 300°F for 3 minutes. Bake until the cheese melts.
4. Serve immediately, topped with a fried egg, if desired.

Nutrition:
Calories: 234
Total Fat: 13 g
Saturated Fat: 7 g
Sodium: 834 mg
Carbohydrates: 16 g
Fiber: 3 g
Protein: 16 g

34. Asparagus Omelet

Preparation Time: 10 minutes
Cooking Time: 8 minutes
Servings: 2

Ingredients:

- 3 eggs
- 5 steamed asparagus tips
- 2 Tbsp. of warm milk
- 1 Tbsp. parmesan cheese, grated
- Salt and pepper, to taste
- Non-stick cooking spray

Directions:

1. In a large bowl combine eggs, cheese, milk, salt, and pepper, then mix until well combined.
2. Spray a baking pan with non-stick cooking spray.
3. Transfer the egg mixture into the pan and add the asparagus, then place the pan inside the baking basket.
4. Set the air fryer to 320°F for 8 minutes.
5. Serve warm.

Nutrition:
Calories: 231
Total Fat: 9.2 g
Carbs: 8 g
Protein: 12.2 g

35. Pumpkin Pie French toast

Preparation Time: 10 minutes
Cooking Time: 20 minutes
Servings: 4

Ingredients:

- 2 large beaten eggs
- 4 slices whole-wheat cinnamon swirl bread
- ¼ cup milk
- ¼ cup pumpkin puree
- ¼ tsp. pumpkin spices
- ¼ cup butter

Directions:

1. In a large mixing bowl, mix milk, eggs, pumpkin puree, and pie spice.

2. Whisk until the mixture is smooth. Dip 2 slices of the bread on both sides in the egg mixture and place on a baking rack.
3. Place the rack inside the air fryer's cooking basket.
4. Set the temperature to 340°F for 10 minutes. Bake until done and repeat with the remaining bread slices.
5. Serve pumpkin pie toast with butter.

Nutrition:
Calories: 212
Total Fat: 8.2 g
Carbs: 7 g
Protein: 11.3 g

36. Breakfast Cheese Bread Cups

Preparation Time: 10 minutes
Cooking Time: 15 minutes
Servings: 2

Ingredients:

- 2 eggs
- 2 Tbsp. cheddar cheese, grated
- Salt and pepper, to taste
- 1 ham slice, cut into 2 pieces
- 4 whole-wheat bread slices, flattened with a rolling pin

Directions:

1. Spray the inside of 2 ramekins with cooking spray.
2. Place 2 flat pieces of bread into each ramekin to form a cup. Add the ham slice pieces into each ramekin.
3. Crack an egg in each ramekin, then sprinkle with cheese. Season with salt and pepper.
4. Place the ramekins into the air fryer at 300°F for 15 minutes.
5. Serve warm.

Nutrition:
Calories: 162
Total Fat: 8 g
Carbs: 10 g
Protein: 11 g

37. Breakfast Cod Nuggets

Preparation Time: 10 minutes
Cooking Time: 10 minutes
Servings: 4

Ingredients:

- 1 lb. cod

For breading:

- 2 eggs, beaten
- 2 Tbsp. olive oil
- 1 cup almond flour
- ¾ cup breadcrumbs
- 1 tsp. dried parsley
- Pinch sea salt
- ½ tsp. black pepper

Directions:

1. Preheat the air fryer to 390°F.
2. Cut the cod into strips about 1-inch by 2-inches. Blend almond flour, olive oil, salt, parsley, and pepper in a food processor.
3. In 3 separate bowls, add breadcrumbs, eggs, and flour.
4. Place each piece of fish into flour, then the eggs, and then the breadcrumbs.
5. Add pieces of cod to the air fryer basket and cook for 10 minutes.
6. Serve warm.

Nutrition:
Calories: 213
Total Fat: 12.6 g
Carbs: 9.2 g
Protein: 13.4 g

38. Vegetable Egg Pancake

Preparation Time: 10 minutes
Cooking Time: 15 minutes
Servings: 2

Ingredients:

- 1 cup almond flour
- ½ cup milk
- 1 Tbsp. parmesan cheese, grated
- 3 eggs
- 1 potato, grated
- 1 beet, peeled and grated
- 1 carrot, grated
- 1 zucchini, grated
- 1 Tbsp. olive oil
- ¼ tsp. nutmeg
- 1 tsp. onion powder
- 1 tsp. garlic powder
- ½ tsp. black pepper

Directions:

1. Preheat your air fryer to 390°F.
2. Mix the zucchini, potato, beet, carrot, eggs, milk, almond flour, and parmesan in a bowl.
3. Place olive oil into an oven-safe dish.
4. Form 4 patties with the vegetable mix and flatten them to form patties.
5. Place patties into an oven-safe dish and cook in the air fryer for 15 minutes.
6. Serve with sliced tomatoes, sour cream, and toast.

Nutrition:
Calories: 223
Total Fat: 11.2 g

Carbs: 10.3 g
Proteins: 13.4 g

39. Oriental Omelet

Preparation Time: 10 minutes
Cooking Time: 12 minutes
Servings: 1

Ingredients:

- ½ cup fresh Shimeji mushrooms, sliced
- 2 eggs, whisked
- Salt and pepper, to taste
- 1 clove garlic, minced
- A handful of sliced tofu
- 2 Tbsp. onion, finely chopped
- Cooking spray

Directions:

1. Spray the baking dish with cooking spray.
2. Add onions and garlic. Air fry in the preheated air fryer at 355°F for 4 minutes.
3. Place the tofu and mushrooms over the onions and add salt and pepper to taste.
4. Whisk the eggs and pour them over tofu and mushrooms.
5. Air fry again for 20 minutes.
6. Serve warm.

Nutrition:
Calories: 210
Total Fat: 11.2 g
Carbs: 8.6 g
Protein: 12.2 g

40. Crispy Breakfast Avocado Fries

Preparation Time: 10 minutes
Cooking Time: 8 minutes
Servings: 2

Ingredients:

- 2 eggs, beaten
- 2 large avocados, peeled, pitted, cut into 8 slices each
- ¼ tsp. pepper
- ½ tsp. cayenne pepper
- Salt, to taste
- Juice of ½ a lemon
- ½ cup whole-wheat flour
- 1 cup whole-wheat breadcrumbs
- Greek yogurt, to serve

Directions:

1. Add flour, salt, pepper, and cayenne pepper to bowl and mix. Add bread crumbs to another bowl. Beat eggs in a third bowl.
2. First, dredge the avocado slices in the flour mixture.
3. Next, dip them into the egg mixture, and finally dredge them in the breadcrumbs.
4. Place avocado fries into the air fryer basket.
5. Preheat the air fryer to 390°F.
6. Place the air fryer basket into the air fryer and cook for 6 minutes.
7. When cook time is completed, transfer the avocado fries onto a serving platter.
8. Sprinkle with lemon juice and serve with Greek yogurt.

Nutrition:
Calories: 272
Total Fat: 13.4 g
Carbs: 11.2 g
Protein: 15.4 g

41. Cheese and Egg Breakfast Sandwich

Preparation Time: 10 minutes
Cooking Time: 6 minutes
Servings: 1

Ingredients:

- 1–2 eggs
- 1–2 slices cheddar or Swiss cheese
- A bit of butter
- 1 roll sliced in half (your choice, Kaiser Bun, English muffin, etc.)

Directions:

1. Butter your sliced roll on both sides.
2. Place the eggs in an oven-safe dish and whisk. Add seasoning if you wish, such as dill, chives, oregano, and salt.
3. Place the egg dish, roll, and cheese into the air fryer.
4. Make assured the buttered sides of the roll are in front of upwards. Set the air fryer to 390°F with a cook time of 6 minutes.
5. Remove the ingredients when cook time is completed by the air fryer.
6. Place the egg and cheese between the pieces of roll and serve warm.
7. You might like to add slices of avocado and tomatoes to this breakfast sandwich!

Nutrition:
Calories: 212
Total Fat: 11.2 g
Carbs: 9.3 g
Protein: 12.4 g

42. Baked Mini Quiche

Preparation Time: 10 minutes
Cooking Time: 15 minutes
Servings: 2

Ingredients:

- 2 eggs
- 1 large yellow onion, diced
- 1 ¾ cups whole-wheat flour
- 1 ½ cups spinach, chopped
- ¾ cup cottage cheese
- Salt and black pepper, to taste
- 2 Tbsp. olive oil
- ¾ cup butter
- ¼ cup milk

Directions:

1. Preheat the air fryer to 355°F. Add the flour, butter, salt, and milk to the bowl and knead the dough until smooth and refrigerate for 15 minutes.
2. Heat a frying pan over medium heat and add the oil to it.
3. When the oil is heated, add the onions into the pan and sauté them. Add spinach to the pan and cook until it wilts.
4. Drain the excess moisture from spinach. Whisk the eggs together, add cheese to the bowl, and mix with the spinach.
5. Take the dough out of the fridge and divide it into eight equal parts. Roll the dough into a ball that will fit into the bottom of the quiche mound. Place the rolled dough into molds and flatten. Place the spinach filling over the dough.
6. Place molds into air fryer basket and place basket inside of air fryer and cook for 15 minutes. Remove quiches from molds and serve warm or cold.

Nutrition:
Calories: 262
Total Fat: 8.2 g
Carbs: 7.3 g
Protein: 9.5 g

43. Peanut Butter and Banana Breakfast Sandwich

Preparation Time: 10 minutes
Cooking Time: 6 minutes
Servings: 1

Ingredients:

- 2 slices whole-wheat bread
- 1 tsp. sugar-free maple syrup
- 1 sliced banana
- 2 Tbsp. peanut butter

Directions:

1. Evenly coat both sides of the slices of bread with peanut butter.
2. Add the sliced banana and drizzle with some sugar-free maple syrup.
3. Heat in the air fryer to 330°F and bake the bread slices for 6 minutes.
4. Serve warm.

Nutrition:
Calories: 211
Total Fat: 8.2 g
Carbs: 6.3 g
Protein: 11.2 g

44. Eggs and Cocotte on Toast

Preparation Time: 10 minutes
Cooking Time: 15 minutes
Servings: 2

Ingredients:

- 1/8 tsp. black pepper
- ¼ tsp. salt
- ½ tsp. Italian seasoning
- ¼ tsp. balsamic vinegar
- ¼ tsp. sugar-free maple syrup
- 1 cup sausages, chopped into small pieces
- 2 eggs
- 2 slices whole-wheat toast
- 3 Tbsp. cheddar cheese, shredded
- 6 slices tomato
- Cooking spray
- A little mayonnaise to serve

Directions:

1. Spray a baking dish with cooking spray. Place the bread slices at the bottom of the dish.
2. Sprinkle the sausages over the bread. Lay the tomatoes over it. Sprinkle the top with cheese.
3. Beat the eggs, and then pour over the top of bread slices. Drizzle vinegar and maple syrup over eggs.
4. Flavor with Italian seasoning, salt, and pepper, then sprinkle some more cheese on top.
5. Place the baking dish in the air fryer basket that should be preheated at 320°F and cook for 10 minutes.
6. Remove from the air fryer and add a touch of mayonnaise and serve.

Nutrition:
Calories: 232
Total Fat: 7.4 g
Carbs: 6.3 g
Protein: 14.2 g

45. Breakfast Frittata

Preparation Time: 10 minutes
Cooking Time: 15 minutes
Servings: 3

Ingredients:

- 6 eggs
- 8 cherry tomatoes, halved
- 2 Tbsp. Parmesan cheese, shredded
- 1 Italian sausage, diced
- Salt and pepper, to taste

Directions:

1. Preheat your air fryer to 355°F. Add the tomatoes and sausage to the baking dish.
2. Place the baking dish into the air fryer and cook for 5 minutes.
3. Meanwhile, add eggs, salt, pepper, cheese, and oil into a mixing bowl, and whisk well.
4. Remove the baking dish from the air fryer and pour the egg mixture on top of the sausage mixture, spreading evenly.
5. Place the dish back into the air fryer and bake for additional 5 minutes.
6. Remove from the air fryer, slice into wedges and serve.

Nutrition:
Calories: 273
Total Fat: 8.2 g
Carbs: 7 g
Protein: 14.2 g

46. Morning Mini Cheeseburger Sliders

Preparation Time: 10 minutes
Cooking Time: 10 minutes
Servings: 6

Ingredients:

- 1 lb. ground beef
- 6 slices cheddar cheese
- 6 whole-wheat dinner rolls
- Salt and black pepper, to taste

Directions:

1. Preheat your air fryer to 390°F.
2. Form 6 beef patties, each about 2.5 oz., and season with salt and black pepper.
3. Add the burger patties to the cooking basket and cook them for 10 minutes.
4. Remove the burger patties from the air fryer, place the cheese on top of burgers, and return to the air fryer and cook for another minute.
5. Remove and put burgers on dinner rolls and serve warm.

Nutrition:
Calories: 262
Total Fat: 9.4 g
Carbs: 8.2 g
Protein: 16.2 g

47. Avocado and Blueberry Muffins

Preparation Time: 10 minutes
Cooking Time: 15 minutes
Servings: 12

Ingredients:

- 2 eggs
- 1 cup blueberries
- 2 cups almond flour
- 1 tsp. baking soda
- 1/8 tsp. salt
- 2 ripe avocados, peeled, pitted, mashed
- 2 Tbsp. liquid Stevia
- 1 cup plain Greek yogurt
- 1 tsp. vanilla extract

For the streusel topping:

- 2 Tbsp. Truvia sweetener
- 4 Tbsp. butter, softened
- 4 Tbsp. almond flour

Directions:

1. Make the streusel topping by mixing Truvia, flour, and butter until you form a crumbly mixture. Place this mixture in the freezer while you make the muffins.
2. Meanwhile, make the muffins by sifting together flour, baking powder, baking soda, and salt, and set aside. Add avocados and liquid Stevia to a bowl and mix well. Adding in one egg at a time, continue to beat. Add the vanilla extract and yogurt and beat again.
3. Add the flour mixture a bit at a time into the avocado mixture and mix well. Add the blueberries into the mixture and gently fold them in. Pour the batter into greased muffin cups until they are half-full.
4. Sprinkle the streusel topping mixture on top of the muffin mixture and place muffin cups in the air fryer basket.
5. Bake in the preheated air fryer at 355°F for 10 minutes. Remove the muffin cups from the air fryer and allow them to cool completely, then serve.

Nutrition:
Calories: 202
Total Fat: 9.2 g
Carbs: 7.2 g
Protein: 6.3 g

48. Cheese Omelets

Preparation Time: 10 minutes
Cooking Time: 15 minutes
Servings: 2

Ingredients:

- 3 eggs
- 1 large yellow onion, diced
- 2 Tbsp. cheddar cheese, shredded
- ½ tsp. soy sauce
- Salt and pepper, to taste
- Olive oil cooking spray

Directions:

1. Spray a small pan that will fit inside of your air fryer with olive oil cooking spray.
2. Transfer onions to the pan and spread them around. Air fry onions for 7 minutes.
3. In a container, whisk together eggs, soy sauce, pepper, and salt.
4. Pour the beaten egg mixture over the cooked onions and sprinkle the top with shredded cheese.
5. Place back into the air fryer and cook for 6 minutes more.
6. Remove from the air fryer and serve omelets with toasted multi-grain bread.

Nutrition:
Calories: 232
Total Fat: 8.2 g
Carbs: 6.2 g
Protein: 12.3 g

49. Cheese and Mushroom Frittata

Preparation Time: 8–10 minutes
Cooking Time: 15 minutes
Servings: 4

Ingredients:

- 4 cups button mushrooms, cut into ¼-inch slices
- 1 large red onion, cut into ¼-inch slices
- 2 Tbsp. olive oil
- 1 tsp. garlic, minced
- 6 eggs
- Salt, to taste
- Ground black pepper, to taste
- 6 Tbsp. feta cheese

Directions:

1. Put the button mushrooms, onions, and garlic in a pan with a Tbsp. of olive oil, and sauté over medium heat for 5 minutes.
2. Transfer to a kitchen towel to dry and cool.
3. Warm up the Air Fryer to 330°F.
4. Place eggs in a bowl and whisk lightly. Flavor with salt and pepper, and then whisk well.
5. Brush the baking dish with olive oil
6. Place sautéed onions and mushrooms in the baking dish, crumble the feta cheese over it, and then pour the eggs on top.
7. Cook for 20 minutes or until a skewer stuck in the middle of the frittata comes out clean.
8. Serve warm.

Nutrition:
Calories: 232
Total Fat: 8.2 g
Carbs: 6.2 g
Protein: 12.3 g

50. Bagels

Preparation Time: 20 minutes
Cooking Time: 15 minutes
Servings: 12

Ingredients:

- ½ lb. whole wheat flour
- 1 tsp. active dry yeast
- 1 tsp. brown sugar
- ½ cup lukewarm water
- 2 Tbsp. butter, softened
- 1 tsp. salt
- 1 large egg

Directions:

1. Dissolve the yeast and sugar in the warm water. Let rest for 5 minutes.
2. Add the remaining ingredients and mix until a sticky dough forms. Cover and let rest for 40 minutes.
3. Knead the dough on a lightly floured surface and divide it into 5 large balls. Let rest for 4 minutes.
4. Preheat air fryer to 360°F.
5. Flatted the dough balls and make a hole in the center of each. Arrange the bagels on a baking sheet lined with parchment paper.
6. Bake for 20 minutes.

Nutrition:
Calories: 232
Total Fat: 8.2 g
Carbs: 6.2 g
Protein: 12.3 g

51. Vegetarian Omelet

Preparation Time: 16 minutes
Cooking Time: 15 minutes
Servings: 2

Ingredients:

- 8 oz. spinach leaves
- 3 spring onions, cut into 1-inch slices
- ½ red bull pepper, cut into 1-inch cubes

- 1 cup button mushrooms, cut into ¼-inch slices
- ½ tsp. ground turmeric
- 1 tsp. thyme
- 1 tsp. salt
- ½ tsp. ground black pepper
- 1 tsp. minced garlic
- 3 Tbsp. olive oil (extra virgin)
- 2 Tbsp. butter
- 1 cup chickpea flour
- 1 cup water

Directions:

1. In a bowl, place spring onions, bell peppers, mushrooms, turmeric, thyme, salt, ground black pepper, minced garlic, and 2 Tbsp. of olive oil. Toss well to combine.
2. Heat a sauté pan over medium-high heat and tip in the vegetable mixture.
3. Sauté for 3 minutes, turning frequently.
4. Add spinach and butter to the pan, and sauté for another 3 minutes, stirring frequently.
5. Remove from the heat and set aside until needed.
6. Place the chickpea flour and water in a bowl, and whisk to smooth batter.
7. Grease the Air Fryer tray with olive oil and pour in the batter.
8. Cook for 3 minutes at 390°F. Flip and cook for another 3 minutes.
9. Transfer fried omelet on a serving plate and top with sautéed vegetables.
10. Serve with salsa on the side.

Nutrition:
Calories: 232
Total Fat: 8.2 g
Carbs: 6.2 g
Protein: 12.3 g

52. Bacon and Cheese Rolls

Preparation Time: 8–10 minutes
Cooking Time: 15 minutes
Servings: 4

Ingredients:

- 1 lb. cheddar cheese, grated
- 1 lb. bacon rashers
- 1 8 oz. can Pillsbury Crescent dough

Directions:

1. Warm up the Air Fryer to 330°F.
2. Cut the bacon rashers into ¼-inch strips and mix with the cheddar cheese. Set aside.
3. Cut the dough sheet to 3 x 3 inch pieces.
4. Place an equal amount of bacon and cheese mixture on the center of the dough pieces and pinch corners together to enclose stuffing.
5. Transfer the parcels in the Air Fry basket and bake for 7 minutes at 330°F.
6. Increase the temperature to 390°F and bake for another 3 minutes.
7. Serve warm.

Nutrition:
Calories: 232
Total Fat: 8.2 g
Carbs: 6.2 g
Protein: 12.3 g

53. Sweet Potato Fritters

Preparation Time: 6–7 minutes
Cooking Time: 15 minutes
Servings: 4

Ingredients:

- 1 can sweet potato puree, 15 oz.
- ½ tsp. minced garlic
- ½ cup frozen spinach, thawed, finely chopped, and drained well
- 1 large leek, minced
- 1 serving flax egg
- ¼ cup almond flour
- ¼ tsp. sweet paprika flakes
- 1 tsp. kosher salt
- ½ tsp. ground white pepper

Directions:

1. Heat the Air Fryer to 330°F.
2. Place all ingredients in a bowl and mix well.
3. Divide into 16 balls and flatten each to a one-inch-thick patty.
4. Place patties in the Air Fryer basket and cook for two minutes at 330°F.
5. Flip and cook for 2 more minutes.
6. If needed, cook in batches.

Nutrition:
Calories: 232
Total Fat: 8.2 g
Carbs: 6.2 g
Protein: 12.3 g

Chapter 4. Appetizer and Sides Recipes

54. Summer Zucchini

Preparation time: 10 minutes
Cooking time: 25 minutes
Servings: 2
Ingredients:

- 1 zucchini, trimmed, sliced
- ¼ tsp. salt
- ½ tsp. white pepper
- 1 tsp. fresh dill, chopped
- 1 Tbsp. canola oil

Directions:

1. In a large bowl combine the sliced zucchini, salt, white pepper, and canola oil. Mix well and transfer the vegetables to the air fryer basket. Flatten them gently.
2. Then close the lid and cook zucchini for 25 minutes at 355°F. Turn the zucchini over every 5 minutes.
3. Transfer the cooked zucchini to plates and top with fresh dill.

Nutrition:
Calories 80
Fat 70.2 g
Fiber 1.3 g
Carbs 3.9 g
Protein 1.4 g

55. Buffalo-Style Cauliflower

Preparation time: 10 minutes
Cooking time: 14 minutes
Servings: 4
Ingredients:

- 2 cups cauliflower florets
- ½ cup Buffalo sauce
- Cooking spray

Directions:

1. In the mixing bowl combine the cauliflower florets and Buffalo sauce.
2. Spray the air fryer basket with cooking spray.
3. Place the cauliflower florets in the air fryer and flatten them gently with a spatula.
4. Close the lid and cook for 14 minutes at 365°F. Flip the cauliflower florets regularly to avoid burning.

Nutrition:
Calories 22
Fat 0.1 g
Fiber 2 g
Carbs 4.2 g
Protein 1 g

56. Asparagus with Nut Oil

Preparation time: 15 minutes
Cooking time: 15 minutes
Servings: 4
Ingredients:

- 10 oz. asparagus
- ½ tsp. salt
- ¼ tsp. ground oregano
- 1 tsp. nut oil

Directions:

1. Trim the asparagus if needed and sprinkle it with salt and ground oregano.
2. Sprinkle the asparagus with nut oil.
3. Transfer the asparagus in the air fryer basket and close the lid.
4. Cook at 350°F for 15 minutes. Turn the asparagus over after 10 minutes of cooking.

Nutrition:
Calories 101
Fat 7.2 g
Fiber 1.5 g
Carbs 3 g
Protein 6.8 g

57. Toasted Buns

Preparation time: 5 minutes
Cooking time: 4 minutes
Servings: 4
Ingredients:

- 4 whole-wheat buns
- 1 egg, beaten
- 1 Tbsp. coconut cream
- ½ tsp. paprika
- ¼ cup almond flour
- Cooking spray

Directions:

1. Mix together the egg with coconut cream and paprika.
2. Dip buns in the egg mixture.
3. Coat them in the almond flour and transfer in the air fryer.
4. Spray with cooking spray and close the lid.
5. Cook the buns for 4 minutes at 395°F.

Nutrition:
Calories 260
Fat 4.1 g
Fiber 2.4 g
Carbs 46.2 g
Protein 9.4 g

58. Chicken Fried Spring Rolls

Preparation Time: 20 minutes
Cooking Time: 10 minutes
Servings: 4

Ingredients:

For the spring roll wrappers:

- 1 egg, beaten
- 8 spring roll wrappers
- 1 tsp. cornstarch
- ½ tsp. olive oil

For the filling:

- 1 cup chicken breast, cooked, shredded
- 1 celery stalk, sliced thinly
- 1 carrot, sliced thinly
- 1 tsp. chicken stock powder, low-sodium
- ½ tsp. ginger, chopped finely
- ½ cup sliced mushrooms

Directions:

1. Preheat the Air Fryer to 390°F.
2. Prepare the filling. In a bowl, combine shredded chicken, mushrooms, carrot and celery. Add in chicken stock powder and ginger. Stir well.
3. Meanwhile, mix cornstarch and egg in a bowl until thick. Set aside.
4. Spoon some filling into a spring roll wrapper. Roll and seal the ends with the egg mixture.
5. Lightly brush spring rolls with oil and place them in the cooking basket.
6. Cook for 4 minutes. Serve.

Nutrition:
Calorie: 150
Carbohydrate: 18 g
Fat: 5 g
Protein: 9 g
Fiber: 1.5 g

59. Sage Spaghetti Squash

Preparation time: 10 minutes
Cooking time: 30 minutes
Servings: 5

Ingredients:

- 1 lb. spaghetti squash, halved
- ½ tsp. sage
- 2 Tbsps. olive oil
- ¼ tsp. salt

Directions:

1. Sprinkle the spaghetti squash halves with sage, salt, and olive oil.
2. Place the squash halves in the air fryer and close the lid.
3. Cook it for 30 minutes at 365°F.
4. When the time is up, transfer the spaghetti squash to a plate and shred it with a fork.
5. Transfer the shredded spaghetti squash to serving plates. Add butter if desired.

Nutrition:
Calories 76
Fat 6.1 g
Fiber 0 g
Carbs 6.3 g
Protein 0.6 g

60. Chili Cabbage Wedges

Preparation time: 10 minutes
Cooking time: 8 minutes
Servings: 4

Ingredients:

- 1 lb. cabbage, cut into wedges
- 4 Tbsps. olive oil
- 3 Tbsps. balsamic vinegar
- 1 tsp. chili flakes
- ¼ tsp. salt

Directions:

1. In the shallow bowl combine together olive oil, balsamic vinegar, chili flakes, and salt.
2. Then brush every cabbage wedge with the oil mixture and transfer in the air fryer in one layer.
3. Cook the cabbage wedges for 5 minutes at 365F.
4. Then flip the vegetables on the other side and cook for 3 minutes more.

Nutrition:
Calories 151
Fat 14.1 g
Fiber 2.9 g
Carbs 6.7 g
Protein 1.5 g

61. Lemon Shredded Cabbage

Preparation time: 10 minutes
Cooking time: 10 minutes
Servings: 2

Ingredients:

- 1 cup white cabbage, shredded
- 1 Tbsp. coconut butter, melted
- ½ tsp. salt
- 1 Tbsp. lemon juice

Directions:

1. Place shredded cabbage in the air fryer and sprinkle it with salt, lemon juice, and coconut butter.
2. Stir the ingredient gently with a fork or spatula.
3. After this, close the lid and cook the cabbage at 375°F for 10 minutes. Stir the shredded cabbage every 2 minutes.

Nutrition:
Calories 61
Fat 5.9 g
Fiber 0.9 g
Carbs 2.2 g
Protein 0.6 g

62. Fried Purple Cabbage

Preparation time: 10 minutes
Cooking time: 12 minutes
Servings: 6
Ingredients:

- 12 oz. purple cabbage
- 2 Tbsps. olive oil
- 1 Tbsp. lemon juice
- ½ tsp. lime zest, grated
- ¼ tsp. chili flakes

Directions:

1. Cut the purple cabbage into small steaks.
2. In a shallow bowl combine together olive oil, lemon juice, chili flakes, and lime zest.
3. Stir the mixture.
4. Brush each cabbage steak with oil mixture and transfer to the air fryer.
5. Cook the cabbage for 12 minutes at 400°F (6 minutes on each side).

Nutrition:
Calories 69
Fat 4.8 g
Fiber 1.6 g
Carbs 7.1 g
Protein 0.9 g

63. Vegetable Burgers

Preparation time: 10 minutes
Cooking time: 20 minutes
Servings: 2
Ingredients:

- 1 small eggplant, peeled
- 1 egg, beaten
- 1 tsp. chives
- ½ tsp. salt
- 1 Tbsp. almond flour
- 1 potato, cooked, mashed
- Cooking spray

Directions:

1. Place the eggplant in the blender and blend until smooth.
2. Add egg, chives, salt, almond flour, and mashed potato.
3. Pulse the mixture for 10 seconds or until homogenous.
4. Spray the air fryer basket with cooking spray.
5. Make small burgers from the eggplant mixture and transfer them to the air fryer.
6. Spray the burgers with cooking spray and close the lid.
7. Cook for 20 minutes at 355°F. Flip the burgers over after 10 minutes of cooking.

Nutrition:
Calories 150
Fat 4.9 g
Fiber 6.7 g
Carbs 21.1 g
Protein 7.1 g

64. Garlic & Cheese Potatoes

Preparation time: 10 minutes
Cooking Time: 40 minutes
Servings: 4
Ingredients:

- 4 Idaho baking potatoes, halved
- 1 Tbsp. garlic powder
- Salt to taste
- ½ cup cheddar cheese, shredded
- 1 tsp. parsley

Directions:

1. Toss all your ingredients in a bowl except cheese.
2. Place potatoes in a baking dish and sprinkle cheese on top.
3. Cook for 40 minutes at 390°F.

Nutrition:
Calories: 498
Total Fat: 19.09g
Carbs: 67.27g
Protein: 16.5g

65. Stuffed Sweet Potato with Spinach

Preparation time: 10 minutes
Cooking Time: 37 minutes
Servings: 4
Ingredients:

- 1 tsp. olive oil
- 1 tsp. lemon zest
- 4 large sweet potatoes
- 1 cup water spinach, steamed, chopped
- 1 Tbsp. tamari sauce
- Salt and pepper to taste
- 3 cloves garlic, minced
- 1 tsp. cumin powder
- 1 tsp. hoisin sauce
- 1 Tbsp. lemon juice

Directions:

1. Wash sweet potatoes, peel and chop them into bite-sized pieces.

2. Add your spinach to a steamer and steam for 2 minutes. In a bowl, combine a tablespoon of tamari sauce, lemon juice, hoisin sauce, minced garlic, cumin powder.
3. Add steamed spinach and season with salt and pepper. Set aside.
4. Preheat your air fryer to 390°F for 5 minutes. Place sweet potatoes in the pan. Drizzle with lemon zest and olive oil.
5. Place into air fryer and cook for 30 minutes. Once cooked slightly open potatoes and add the spinach mixture to them. Cook for another 5 minutes and serve warm.

Nutrition:
Calories: 114
Total Fat: 0.07g
Carbs: 26.76g
Protein: 2.09g

66. Black Beans & Cauliflower Burgers

Preparation time: 10 minutes
Cooking Time: 15 minutes
Servings: 4
Ingredients:

- 3 cloves garlic, minced
- 1 Tbsp. basil leaves, minced
- 1 tsp. olive oil
- 1 tsp. chili sauce
- 1 Tbsp. vegan oyster sauce
- ¾ cup vegan mayonnaise
- 4 large tomatoes, sliced
- 2 Tbsps. potato starch
- 1 Tbsp. flaxseed mixed with 3 Tbsps. water
- 1 cup black beans
- 1 large head cauliflower, cut into florets
- 1 Tbsp. rice vinegar
- 1 large avocado, mashed

Directions:

1. Cut the cauliflower, then soak it in a pot of warm water for a couple of minutes. Soak black beans in pot of warm water with cauliflower. Rinse with cold water, then pat dry.
2. Add vegan oyster sauce, rice vinegar, chili sauce, and olive oil into food processor and season with salt and pepper. Add basil leaves and garlic. Blend until the mixture becomes rice-like in consistency.
3. Transfer the mixture to a bowl and set aside. Clean the food processor, then add flax seed and 3 tablespoons of water and blend mixture until it becomes fluffy. Transfer this mixture to the bowl with cauliflower mixture, add potato starch and toss to blend ingredients.
4. Shape burger mixture into big balls and flatten on a baking sheet to make burger patties.
5. Preheat your air fryer to 360°F for 2 minutes. Place burger patties in the air-fryer basket. Cook for 15 minutes. Make sure to flip the patties halfway through the cook time.
6. Prepare the tomatoes and cut avocado into halves and remove the pit. Scoop the avocado flesh and mash in a bowl with a fork. Use the veggie burgers as buns. Start with one veggie burger at the bottom, followed by mashed avocado, then a slice of tomato.
7. Spread some vegan mayonnaise on top of tomato and cover with another veggie burger. Serve warm.

Nutrition:
Calories: 124
Total Fat: 4.41g
Carbs: 9.99g
Protein: 10.99g

67. Pomelo Herb Salad with Air-Fried Brussels Sprouts

Preparation time: 10 minutes
Cooking Time: 20 minutes
Servings: 5
Ingredients:

- 1 tsp. olive oil
- Salt and pepper to taste
- 1 large pomelo, peeled
- 2 cups Brussels sprouts, cut into halves
- 1 tablespoon basil leaves, chopped
- 1 Tbsp. parsley, chopped
- 1 Tbsp. vegan oyster sauce
- 2 Tbsps. rice vinegar
- 1 Tbsp. cilantro leaves, chopped

Directions:

1. Wash pomelo, Brussels sprouts, basil, cilantro leaves. Pat dry.
2. Peel the outer and inner skin from pomelo, leaving the pulp. Cut pulp into small bite-size pieces. Set aside.
3. Chop parsley and basil. In a bowl, combine pomelo, basil, parsley. Add rice vinegar and sprinkle with pepper. Mix all ingredients well.
4. In another mixing bowl, combine Brussels sprouts, thyme powder, vegan oyster sauce, toss and allow to soak for 30 minutes.

5. Preheat your air fryer to 360°F. Spray a teaspoon of olive oil over Brussels sprouts in air fryer, then cook them for 20 minutes. Once cooked, add the Brussels sprouts to the bowl with pomelo herb salad and toss to blend ingredients. Serve right away!

Nutrition:
Calories: 46
Total Fat: 0.54g
Carbs: 9.2g
Protein: 3.48g

68. Parmesan Zucchini Chips

Preparation Time: 20 minutes
Cooking Time: 20 minutes
Servings: 4
Ingredients:

- 1 oz. pork rinds
- ½ cup grated Parmesan cheese
- 2 medium zucchini
- 1 large egg

Directions:

1. Slice zucchini into ¼-inch-thick slices. Place between two layers of paper towels or a clean kitchen towel for 30 minutes to remove excess moisture.
2. Place pork rinds into food processor and pulse until finely ground. Pour into a medium bowl and mix with Parmesan.
3. Beat egg in a small bowl.
4. Dip zucchini slices in egg and then in pork rind mixture, coating completely on all sides. Carefully place each slice into the air fryer basket in a single layer, working in batches as necessary.
5. Adjust temperature to 320°F and set the timer for 10 minutes. Flip chips halfway through the cooking time. Serve warm.

Nutrition:
Calories: 121
Protein: 9.9g
Fiber: 0.6g
Fat: 6.7g
Carbs: 3.8g

69. Confit Cherry Tomatoes

Preparation Time: 10 minutes
Cooking Time: 20 minutes
Servings: 1
Ingredients:

- 100 g cherry tomatoes
- 20 ml olive oil
- The grated rind of half a lemon
- 1 Tbsp. grated orange peel
- 1 small garlic clove
- 10 g brown sugar
- Salt, to taste

Directions:

1. Wash and dry the cherry tomatoes and then cut them in half.
2. Place a sheet of baking paper in the bottom of the air fryer. Place the cherry tomatoes in the basket of the air fryer, cut-side up.
3. Peel and wash the garlic clove and mince it.
4. In a bowl, put the oil, sugar, salt, orange and lemon peel and garlic. Mix well and then sprinkle the cherry tomatoes with the mixture.
5. Close the basket and bake at 160°C for 10 minutes.
6. After 10 minutes, increase the temperature to 180°C and continue cooking for another 5 minutes.
7. After 5 minutes, increase the temperature again to 200°C and continue for another 5 minutes.
8. Once they are cooked, remove the cherry tomatoes from the air fryer.
9. Place the confit cherry tomatoes on a plate and serve.

Nutrition :
Calories: 120
Carbohydrates: 12 g
Fats: 9 g
Protein: 2 g

70. Leeks and Ham

Preparation Time: 20 minutes
Cooking Time: 25 minutes
Servings: 1
Ingredients:

- 1 large leek
- 40 g sliced cooked ham
- 2 slices emmenthal cheese
- 1 whole egg
- 1 egg yolk
- 50 ml milk
- 1 pinch nutmeg
- Salt and pepper, to taste
- Olive oil, to taste

Directions:

1. Remove the end and outer leaves from the leek, wash and then cut it in half lengthwise.
2. Blanch the leek in boiling salted water for 5 minutes then drain and allow to cool.
3. Wrap each leek half with a slice of cheese and then in a slice of ham.
4. Place the leeks in a pan brushed with olive oil.
5. Place the egg in a bowl. Add the yolk and beat them with a fork. Add milk, nutmeg, pepper, and salt.

6. Stir well and then pour the mixture over the leeks and spread the remaining cheese slices on top. Place the pan inside the air fryer and bake at 170°C for 20 minutes.
7. When done, remove the pan from the air fryer. Place the leeks in a dish and serve.

Nutrition:
Calories: 228
Carbohydrates: 12 g
Fats: 13 g
Protein: 15 g

71. Potato Scones

Preparation Time: 20 minutes
Cooking Time: 15 minutes
Servings: 1
Ingredients:

- 50 g pre-boiled potatoes
- 50 g whole-wheat flour
- 1 tsp. instant yeast
- 10 g butter
- Olive oil, to taste
- Salt and pepper, to taste

Directions:

1. Peel the boiled potatoes and then cut them into cubes. Put in a bowl and mash them with a fork.
2. Put the flour, baking powder, butter, salt and pepper in another bowl. Knead with your fingertips until the mixture has a sandy consistency.
3. Add the mashed potatoes and continue kneading for another 4 minutes.
4. Place the dough on a lightly floured work surface and roll it out into a 2 cm thick sheet.
5. With the help of a round pastry cutter, form dough disks of about 5 cm in diameter.
6. Place the disks inside the air fryer and bake at 180° for 15 minutes, turning them halfway through cooking.
7. When they are cooked, remove the potato scones from the air fryer, place them on a serving plate and serve.

Nutrition :
Calories: 182
Carbohydrates: 24 g
Fats: 8 g
Protein: 4 g

72. Cauliflower Rosti

Preparation Time: 15 minutes
Cooking Time: 8 minutes
Servings: 1
Ingredients:

- 100 g cauliflower florets
- 1 small clove of garlic, minced
- 1 egg
- Dried oregano, to taste
- Salt and pepper, to taste
- Olive oil, to taste

Directions:

1. Wash and dry the cauliflower florets and then grate them with a large hole grater.
2. Transfer to a bowl and season with salt, oregano, pepper and chopped garlic. Add the egg and mix well with a spoon.
3. When everything is well mixed, take some of the mixture with your hands and form it into a ball, then flatten it into a patty.
4. Place the rosti inside the air fryer and spray it with a little olive oil.
5. Bake at 180°C for 3 minutes, then turn them over, drizzle with a little more oil and continue cooking for another 5 minutes.
6. When the cooking is finished, remove the rosti from the air fryer, place them on a serving plate and serve.

Nutrition :
Calories: 76
Carbohydrates: 5 g
Fats: 6 g
Protein: 2 g

73. Mushroom Puffs

Preparation Time: 20 minutes
Cooking Time: 20 minutes
Servings: 1
Ingredients:

- 70 g puff pastry
- 70 g mixed mushrooms
- 20 g chopped onion
- ½ cup mozzarella
- 10 g grated Parmesan cheese
- Salt and pepper, to taste
- Olive oil, to taste

Directions:

1. Place the puff pastry on a lightly floured work surface and roll it out with a rolling pin. Cut the puff pastry into 2 rectangles of the size you desire.
2. Remove the ends of the mushrooms, rinse them under running water, dry them well and then slice them.

3. Heat a little oil in a pan and sauté the onion. When it has wilted, add the mushrooms, and cook for 10 minutes over medium-high heat. Adjust the salt and pepper and remove from the heat.
4. Cut the mozzarella into cubes. Place the mushrooms and mozzarella in the center of each puff pastry rectangle.
5. Sprinkle with grated Parmesan cheese and then brush the edges of the pastry with a little beaten egg yolk. Fold in half and ensure the puffs are sealed.
6. Place inside the air fryer and bake at 180°C for 10 minutes.
7. When the cooking is finished, remove the puffs from the air fryer, place them on a serving plate and serve.

Nutrition :
Calories: 234
Carbohydrates: 18 g
Fats: 4 g
Protein: 8 g

74. Courgette and Brie Puff Pastry

Preparation Time: 20 minutes
Cooking TIme: 15 minutes
Servings: 1
Ingredients:

- 60 g puff pastry
- 25 g Brie
- ½ courgette (zucchini)
- Salt and pepper, to taste
- Olive oil, as required.

Directions:

1. Peel the courgette, wash it and then cut it into fairly thin rounds. Cut the brie into thin slices.
2. Place the puff pastry on a lightly floured work surface and roll it out with a rolling pin. With a pastry cutter, cut out squares of dough.
3. Place the puff pastry inside a baking tin brushed with olive oil. Place slices of brie cheese on the base of each pastry sheet. Finally, add the courgette slices. Adjust salt and pepper and place the baking tin inside the air fryer.
4. Bake at 200°C for 15 minutes, checking often.
5. When done, remove the pan from the air fryer and let it cool.
6. Once cooled, place them on a serving plate and serve.

Nutrition :
Calories: 426
Carbohydrates: 32 g
Fats: 14 g
Protein: 8 g

75. Pea and Spring Onion Flans

Preparation Time: 20 minutes
Cooking Time: 23 minutes
Servings: 1
Ingredients:

- 10 g grated Parmesan cheese
- 25 g spring onions
- 10 g butter
- 50 g peas
- 1 egg
- 1 pinch of nutmeg
- 2 Tbsps. fresh cream
- Salt and pepper, to taste
- Olive oil, as required

Directions:

1. Wash and dry the spring onion and slice it.
2. Brush a single-portion baking tin with olive oil and place the spring onion, peas, and butter inside.
3. Place the pan inside the air fryer and bake at 180°C for 5 minutes.
4. When done, remove the pan from the air fryer, stir well and then let cool. Add the egg, cream, grated Parmesan cheese, salt, pepper, and nutmeg to the pan. Mix well.
5. Place the pan inside the air fryer and bake at 180°C for 18 minutes.
6. When done, remove the pan from the air fryer and let it rest for 5 minutes.
7. Turn the flan upside down on the serving plate and serve.

Nutrition:
Calories: 185
Carbohydrates: 8 g
Fats: 10 g
Protein: 6 g

76. Pumpkin and Taleggio Cheese Flans

Preparation Time: 20 minutes
Cooking Time: 30 minutes
Servings: 1
Ingredients:

- 200 g pumpkin, peeled and deseeded
- 50 g fresh ricotta
- 25 g Parmesan cheese
- 15 g Taleggio cheese
- 10 g butter
- 10 g whole-wheat flour
- 25 ml milk
- 1 beaten egg
- A pinch of nutmeg
- Salt and pepper, to taste
- Olive oil, as required

Directions:

1. Wash the pumpkin and cut it into cubes. Put the butter in a non-stick pan and melt it. Add the pumpkin and mix well. Cover with a lid and stew the pumpkin for 15 minutes.
2. Remove the lid, adjust the salt and pepper and cook for a further 2 minutes so that the pumpkin dries out completely.
3. Switch off, place the pumpkin in the blender and blend it to a puree.
4. Put the pumpkin in a bowl and add the flour. Stir well and then add the milk in a trickle. Stir until smooth. Finally, mix in nutmeg, salt, pepper, ricotta, Parmesan, diced taleggio cheese and beaten egg.
5. Pour the mixture into small metal flan molds.
6. Place the molds inside the air fryer and bake at 180°C for 15 minutes.
7. When done, remove the molds from the air fryer and let them cool.
8. Turn the flans upside down and serve.

Nutrition:
Calories: 372
Carbohydrates: 17 g
Fats: 16 g
Protein: 21 g

77. Broccoli Casserole

Preparation Time: 30 minutes
Cooking Time: 27 minutes
Servings: 1
Ingredients:

- 60 ml béchamel sauce
- 50 g broccoli
- 1 egg
- 15 g grated Parmesan cheese
- Olive oil, as required.
- Salt and pepper, to taste

Directions:

1. Start by cutting the broccoli into small florets. Wash and dry them. Put the broccoli in a pot with salted water and cook for 8 minutes.
2. Drain the broccoli. Heat a little olive oil in a frying pan. When the oil is hot enough, fry the broccoli for 4 minutes. Season with salt and pepper and then transfer the broccoli into a blender. Blend until thick and smooth.
3. Transfer the broccoli cream into a bowl.
4. Separate the egg. Put the yolk in the bowl with the broccoli and the egg white in another bowl.
5. Whip the egg white until stiff.
6. In the bowl with the broccoli and yolks, add the béchamel sauce, Parmesan cheese and a pinch of salt and pepper. Mix everything together. Add the egg whites and gently fold it into the mixture.
7. Pour the mixture into a single-portion mold brushed with olive oil, filling it ¾ of the way.
8. Place the mold in the air fryer and bake at 180°C for 15 minutes.
9. Once cooked, remove it from the fryer and serve immediately.

Nutrition:
Calories: 210
Carbohydrates: 20 g
Fats: 10 g
Protein: 7 g

78. Garlic Kale Chips

Preparation Time: 6–7 minutes
Cooking Time: 10 minutes
Servings: 2
Ingredients:

- 1 Tbsp. yeast flakes
- Sea salt, to taste
- 1 tsp. vegan seasoning
- 4 cups packed kale
- 2 Tbsp. olive oil
- 1 tsp. garlic, minced

Directions:

1. In a bowl, place the oil, kale, garlic, and ranch seasoning. Add the yeast and mix well.
2. Place the coated kale into the air fryer basket and cook at 375°F for 5 minutes.
3. Shake after 3 minutes and serve.

Nutrition:
Calories: 50
Total Fat: 1.9 g
Carbs: 10 g
Protein: 46 g

79. Garlic Salmon Balls

Preparation Time: 6–7 minutes
Cooking Time: 10 minutes
Servings: 2
Ingredients:

- 6 oz. canned salmon, drained
- 1 large egg
- 3 Tbsp. olive oil
- 5 Tbsp. wheat germ
- ½ tsp. garlic powder
- 1 Tbsp. fresh dill, chopped
- 4 Tbsp. spring onion, diced
- 4 Tbsp. celery, diced

Directions:

1. Preheat your air fryer to 370°F.

2. In a large bowl, mix the salmon, egg, celery, onion, dill, and garlic.
3. Shape the mixture into golf ball size balls and roll them in the wheat germ.
4. Add the salmon balls to the air fryer pan and flatten them. Spray them with olive oil.
5. Transfer the pan to your air fryer and cook for 10 minutes.

Nutrition:
Calories: 219
Total Fat: 7.7 g
Carbs: 14.8 g
Protein: 23.1 g

80. Onion Rings

Preparation Time: 7 minutes
Cooking Time: 10 minutes
Servings: 3

Ingredients:

- 1 onion
- 1 ½ cups almond flour
- ¾ cup pork rinds, crumbed
- 1 cup milk
- 1 egg
- 1 Tbsp. baking powder
- ½ tsp. salt

Directions:

1. Preheat your air fryer for 10 minutes.
2. Cut onion into slices, then separate into rings. In a container, mix the flour, baking powder, and salt.
3. Whisk the eggs and the milk, and combines with the flour mixture.
4. Gently dip the floured onion rings into the batter to coat them.
5. Spread the pork rinds on a plate and dredge the rings in the crumbs.
6. Place the onion rings in your air fryer and cook for 10 minutes at 360°F.

Nutrition:
Calories: 304
Total Fat: 18 g
Carbs: 31 g
Protein: 38 g

81. Crispy Eggplant Fries

Preparation Time: 7 minutes
Cooking Time: 12 minutes
Servings: 3

Ingredients:

- 2 eggplants
- ¼ cup olive oil
- ¼ cup almond flour
- ½ cup water

Directions:

1. Preheat your air fryer to 390°F.
2. Cut the eggplants into half-inch slices. In a mixing bowl, mix the flour, olive oil, water, and eggplants and mix well to coat the eggplants evenly.
3. Add eggplants to the air fryer and cook for 12 minutes.
4. Serve with yogurt or tomato sauce.

Nutrition:
Calories: 103
Total Fat: 7.3 g
Carbs: 12.3 g
Protein: 1.9 g

82. Charred Bell Peppers

Preparation Time: 7 minutes
Cooking Time: 4 minutes
Servings: 3

Ingredients:

- 2 bell peppers, sliced and seeded
- 1 tsp. olive oil
- 1 pinch sea salt
- 1 lemon

Directions:

1. Preheat your air fryer to 390°F. Sprinkle the peppers with oil and salt.
2. Cook the peppers in the air fryer for 4 minutes.
3. Place peppers in a large bowl and squeeze lemon juice over the top.
4. Season with salt and pepper.

Nutrition:
Calories: 30
Total Fat: 0.25 g
Carbs: 6.91 g
Protein: 1.28 g

83. Garlic Tomatoes

Preparation Time: 7 minutes
Cooking Time: 15 minutes
Servings: 4

Ingredients:

- 3 Tbsp. vinegar
- ½ tsp. thyme, dried
- 4 tomatoes
- 1 Tbsp. olive oil
- Salt and black pepper, to taste
- 1 clove garlic, minced

Directions:

1. Preheat your air fryer to 390°F. Cut the tomatoes into halves and remove the seeds.

2. Place them in a big bowl and toss them with oil, salt, pepper, garlic, and thyme.
3. Place them into the air fryer and cook for 15 minutes.
4. Drizzle with vinegar and serve.

Nutrition:
Calories: 28.9
Total Fat: 2.4 g
Carbs: 2.0 g
Protein: 0.4 g

84. Mushroom Stew

Preparation Time: 7 minutes
Cooking Time: 1 hour and 22 minutes
Servings: 6

Ingredients:

- 1 lb. chicken, boneless, skinless
- 2 Tbsp. canola oil
- 1 lb. fresh mushrooms, sliced
- 1 Tbsp. thyme, dried
- ¾ cup water
- 2 Tbsp. tomato paste
- 3 large tomatoes, chopped
- 4 cloves garlic, minced
- 1 cup green peppers, sliced
- 3 cups zucchini, diced
- 1 large onion, diced
- 1 Tbsp. basil
- 1 Tbsp. marjoram
- 1 Tbsp. oregano

Directions:

1. Preheat your air fryer to 390°F. Cut the chicken into cubes. Position them in the air fryer basket and spray olive oil over them.
2. Add mushrooms, zucchini, onion, tomatoes, and green pepper. Mix and add in garlic, tomato paste, water, and seasonings.
3. Lock the air fryer and cook the stew for 50 minutes.
4. Set the heat to 340°F and cook for an additional 20 minutes.
5. Remove from air fryer, transfer into a large serving dish and serve.

Nutrition:
Calories: 53
Total Fat: 3.3 g
Carbs: 4.9 g
Protein: 2.3 g

85. Cheese and Onion Nuggets

Preparation Time: 7 minutes
Cooking Time: 12 minutes
Servings: 4

Ingredients:

- 7 oz. Edam cheese, grated
- 2 spring onions, diced
- 1 egg, beaten
- 1 Tbsp. coconut oil
- 1 Tbsp. dried thyme
- Salt and pepper, to taste

Directions:

1. Mix the onion, cheese, coconut oil, salt, pepper, and thyme in a bowl.
2. Make 8 small balls.
3. Put them in the fridge for about an hour.
4. With a pastry brush, carefully brush beaten egg over the nuggets.
5. Cook for 12 minutes in the air fryer at 350°F.

Nutrition:
Calories: 227
Total Fat: 17.3 g
Carbs: 4.5 g
Protein: 14.2 g

86. Spiced Nuts

Preparation Time: 7 minutes
Cooking Time: 10 minutes
Servings: 3 cups

Ingredients:

- 1 cup almonds
- 1 cup pecan halves
- 1 cup cashews
- 1 egg white, beaten
- ½ tsp. ground cinnamon
- Pinch cayenne pepper
- ¼ tsp. ground cloves
- Pinch of salt

Directions:

1. Combine the egg white with spices.
2. Preheat your air fryer to 300°F. Toss the nuts in the spiced mixture. Transfer to the air fryer pan.
3. Cook for 10 minutes, stirring several times throughout the cooking time.

Nutrition:
Calories: 88.4
Total Fat: 7.6 g
Carbs: 3.9 g
Protein: 2.5 g

87. Keto French fries

Preparation Time: 7 minutes
Cooking Time: 20 minutes
Servings: 4

Ingredients:

- 1 large rutabaga, peeled, cut into spears about ¼-inch wide
- Salt and pepper, to taste
- ½ tsp. paprika
- 2 Tbsp. coconut oil

Directions:

1. Preheat your air fryer to 450°F.
2. Mix the oil, paprika, salt, and pepper.
3. Pour the oil mixture over the fries, making sure all pieces are well coated.
4. Cook in the air fryer for 20 minutes or until crispy. Shake the basket half way through the cooking time.

Nutrition:
Calories: 113
Total Fat: 7.2 g
Carbs: 12.5 g
Protein: 1.9 g

88. Fried Garlic Green Tomatoes

Preparation Time: 7 minutes
Cooking Time: 12 minutes
Servings: 2

Ingredients:

- 3 green tomatoes, sliced
- ½ cup almond flour
- 2 eggs, beaten
- Salt and pepper, to taste
- 1 tsp. garlic, minced

Directions:

1. Season the tomatoes with salt, garlic, and pepper.
2. Preheat your air fryer to 400°F.
3. Dip the tomatoes first in flour, then in the egg mixture. Spray the tomato rounds with olive oil and place them in the air fryer basket.
4. Cook for 8 minutes, then flip over and cook for additional 4 minutes.
5. Serve with zero-carb mayonnaise.

Nutrition:
Calories: 123
Total Fat: 3.9 g
Carbs: 16 g
Protein: 8.4 g

89. Garlic Cauliflower Tots

Preparation Time: 7 minutes
Cooking Time: 20 minutes
Servings: 6

Ingredients:

- 1 head cauliflower, cut into florets and chopped in a food processor
- ½ cup Parmesan cheese, grated
- Salt and pepper, to taste
- ¼ cup almond flour
- 2 eggs
- 1 tsp. garlic, minced

Directions:

1. Mix all the ingredients. Shape into tots and spray with olive oil.
2. Preheat your air fryer to 400°F.
3. Cook for 10 minutes on each side.

Nutrition:
Calories: 18
Total Fat: 0.6 g
Carbs: 1.3 g
Protein: 1.8 g

90. Green Onions and Parmesan Tomatoes

Preparation Time: 7 minutes
Cooking Time: 15 minutes
Servings: 4

Ingredients:

- 4 large tomatoes, cut into slices
- 1 Tbsp. olive oil
- Salt and pepper, to taste
- ½ tsp. thyme, dried
- 2 garlic cloves, minced
- 2 green onions, finely chopped
- ½ cup Parmesan, freshly grated

Directions:

1. Preheat your air fryer to 390°F.
2. Coat the tomato slices with olive oil, season with garlic, thyme, salt, and pepper.
3. Top with Parmesan and chopped green onions.
4. Place tomatoes in the air fryer and cook for 15 minutes.
5. Serve on top of crostini or any meat, poultry, or fish.

Nutrition:
Calories: 69
Total Fat: 3.9 g
Carbs: 69 g
Protein: 1.6 g

91. Green Bell Peppers with Cauliflower Stuffing

Preparation Time: 7 minutes
Cooking Time: 20 minutes
Servings: 4

Ingredients:

- 4 green bell peppers, top cut, deseeded
- 1 tsp. lemon juice
- 2 Tbsp. coriander leaves, finely chopped
- 2 green chilies, finely chopped
- 2 cups cauliflower, cooked and mashed
- 2 onions, finely chopped
- 1 tsp. cumin seeds
- ¼ tsp. turmeric powder
- ¼ tsp. chili powder
- ¼ tsp. garam masala
- Salt, to taste
- Olive oil, as needed

Directions:

1. In a saucepan, heat the oil and sauté the chilies, onion, and cumin seeds.
2. Add the rest of the ingredients except the bell peppers and mix well.
3. Preheat your air fryer to 390°F for 10 minutes.
4. Brush the green bell peppers with olive oil, inside and out, and stuff each pepper with cauliflower mixture.
5. Place them into the air fryer and grill for 10 minutes.

Nutrition:
Calories: 257
Total Fat: 4.0 g
Carbs: 44.8 g
Protein: 12.3 g

92. Cheesy Chickpea and Courgette Burgers

Preparation Time: 7 minutes
Cooking Time: 10 minutes
Servings: 4

Ingredients:

- 1 can chickpeas, drained and mashed
- 3 Tbsp. fresh coriander
- 1 oz. cheddar cheese, shredded
- 2 eggs, beaten
- 1 tsp. garlic paste
- 1 zucchini grated
- 1 red onion, diced
- 1 tsp. chili powder
- 1 tsp. mixed spice
- Salt and pepper, to taste
- 1 tsp. cumin

Directions:

1. Mix your ingredients in a mixing bowl.
2. Shape portions of the mixture into burger patties.
3. Place in the air fryer and bake at 300°F for 15 minutes.

Nutrition:
Calories: 184.8
Total Fat: 10.1 g,
Carbs: 18.4 g
Protein: 13.2 g

93. Spicy Sweet Potatoes

Preparation Time: 7 minutes
Cooking Time: 23 minutes
Servings: 4

Ingredients:

- 3 sweet potatoes, peeled and chopped into chips
- 1 tsp. chili powder
- 1 tsp. paprika
- 2 Tbsp. olive oil
- 1 Tbsp. red wine vinegar
- 1 tomato, thinly sliced
- ½ cup tomato sauce
- 1 onion, peeled and diced
- Salt and pepper, to taste
- 1 tsp. rosemary
- 1 tsp. oregano
- 1 tsp. mixed spice
- 2 tsp. thyme
- 2 tsp. fresh coriander

Directions:

1. Toss the chips in a bowl with olive oil, chili powder and paprika.
2. Add to the air fryer and cook for 15 minutes at 360°F.
3. Mix the remaining ingredients in a baking dish.
4. Cook the sauce in the air fryer for 8 minutes.
5. Toss the potatoes in the sauce and serve warm.

Nutrition:
Calories: 303
Total Fat: 5 g
Carbs: 57 g
Protein: 8 g

94. Olives, Cheese, and Broccoli

Preparation Time: 7 minutes
Cooking Time: 15 minutes
Servings: 4

Ingredients:

- 2 lbs. broccoli florets
- 2 Tbsp. olive oil

- ¼ cup Parmesan cheese shaved
- 2 tsp. lemon zest, grated
- 1/3 cup Kalamata olives (halved, pitted)
- ½ tsp. ground black pepper
- 1 tsp. sea salt

Directions:

1. Boil water in a pan over medium heat and cook the broccoli for about 4 minutes. Drain.
2. Mix the broccoli with salt, pepper, and olive oil in a bowl.
3. Place in the air fryer and cook at 400°F for 15 minutes. Toss twice during cook time.
4. Move to a dish and toss with lemon zest, cheese, and olives.

Nutrition:
Calories: 214
Total Fat: 13.45 g
Carbs: 13.22 g
Protein: 12.56 g

95. Veggie Mix

Preparation Time: 7 minutes
Cooking Time: 35 minutes
Servings: 4

Ingredients:

- ½ lb. carrots, peeled, cubed
- 6 tsp. olive oil
- ½ tsp. tarragon leaves
- ½ tsp. white pepper
- Salt, to taste
- 1 lb. yellow squash, chopped into wedges
- 1 lb. zucchini, chopped into wedges

Directions:

1. Mix the carrots with 2 tsp. of olive oil in your air fryer basket. Cook at 400°F for 5 minutes.
2. Add in the squash and zucchini along with the rest of the oil, salt, and pepper into the air fryer.
3. Cook for additional 30 minutes, tossing twice during cook time.
4. Mix with tarragon and serve.

Nutrition:
Calories: 162
Total Fat: 1.2 g
Carbs: 30.3 g
Protein: 7.5 g

96. Garlic and Cheese Potatoes

Preparation Time: 7 minutes
Cooking Time: 40 minutes
Servings: 4

Ingredients:

- 4 Idaho baking potatoes, halved
- 1 Tbsp. garlic powder
- Salt, to taste
- ½ cup cheddar cheese, shredded
- 1 tsp. parsley

Directions:

1. Toss all your ingredients in a bowl except cheese.
2. Place potatoes in a baking dish and sprinkle cheese over top of them.
3. Cook in the air fryer for 40 minutes at 390°F.

Nutrition:
Calories: 498
Total Fat: 19.09 g
Carbs: 67.27 g
Protein: 16.5 g

97. Garlic Baby Potatoes

Preparation Time: 7 minutes
Cooking Time: 10 minutes
Servings: 2

Ingredients:

- 8 oz. boiled baby potatoes
- ½ tsp. sesame seeds
- Red chili powder, to taste
- Salt and pepper, to taste
- ½ tsp. garlic paste
- ¼ tsp. coriander seeds, dry roasted
- ¼ tsp. cumin seeds, dry roasted
- ½ cup. fresh cream

Directions:

1. Grind the coriander and cumin seeds to form a powder. Toss all the ingredients in a baking dish except the cream.
2. Preheat your air fryer for 5 minutes at 360°F. Cook potatoes for 5 minutes.
3. Mix in cream and air fry for an additional 5 minutes.
4. Garnish with sesame seeds.

Nutrition:
Calories: 498
Total Fat: 19.09 g
Carbs: 67.27 g
Protein: 16.5 g

Chapter 5. Meat Recipes

98. Glazed Ham

Preparation Time: 15 minutes
Cooking Time: 40 minutes
Servings: 4
Ingredients:

- 1½ lb. ham
- 1 cup whiskey
- 2 Tbsps. French mustard
- 2 Tbsps. honey

Directions:

1. Place the ham at room temperature for about 30 minutes before cooking.
2. In a bowl, mix together the whiskey, mustard, and honey.
3. Place the ham in a baking dish that fits in the air fryer.
4. Top with half of the honey mixture and coat well.
5. Set the temperature of air fryer to 320°F. Place the baking dish into the air fryer.
6. Air fry for about 15 minutes.
7. Flip the side of ham and top with the remaining honey mixture.
8. Air fry for about 25 minutes more.
9. Remove from air fryer and place the ham onto a platter for about 10 minutes to rest before slicing.
10. Cut the ham into desired size slices and serve.

Nutrition:
Calories: 558
Carbohydrate: 18.6g
Protein: 43g
Fat: 22.2g
Sugar: 8.7g
Sodium: 3000mg

99. Simple Lamb Chops

Preparation Time: 10 minutes
Cooking Time: 6 minutes
Servings: 4
Ingredients

- 1 Tbsp. olive oil
- Salt and ground black pepper, as required
- 4 (4 oz. each) lamb chops

Directions:

1. In a large bowl, mix together the oil, salt, and black pepper.
2. Add the chops and coat evenly with the mixture.
3. Set the temperature of air fryer to 390°F. Grease an air fryer basket.
4. Arrange chops into the prepared air fryer basket in a single layer.
5. Air fry for about 5-6 minutes.
6. Remove from air fryer and transfer the chops onto plates.
7. Serve hot.

Nutrition:
Calories: 486
Carbohydrate: 0.8g
Protein: 63.8g
Fat: 31.7g
Sugar: 0g
Sodium: 250mg

100. Lamb Chops with Cherry Tomatoes and Green Olives

Preparation Time: 15 minutes
Cooking Time: 16 minutes
Servings: 4
Ingredients:

- 2 lamb chops (100 g each)
- 2 cloves garlic
- 6 cherry tomatoes
- 1 tsp. oregano
- 1 Tbsp. chopped green olives
- 30 ml red wine
- Olive oil, as required
- Salt and pepper, to taste

Directions:

1. Wash and dry the cherry tomatoes and then cut them in half. Peel the garlic cloves and then chop.
2. Wash the lamb chops, remove excess fat, and then pat them dry with paper towels. Brush the ribs with oil and then sprinkle them with salt and pepper.
3. Place the chops in a pan suitable for your air fryer. Place the cherry tomatoes inside and then sprinkle with salt, pepper, garlic, oregano and chopped olives.
4. Cook the chops for 8 minutes at 180°C, then turn them over, drizzle with red wine and continue cooking for a further 8 minutes.
5. Oncce done, remove the chops from the fryer.
6. Place the chops, olives and cherry tomatoes in a serving dish, sprinkle with the cooking juices and serve.

Nutrition:
Calories: 390
Carbohydrates 10 g
Fats: 11 g
Protein: 38 g

101. Lamb Chops with Herbs and Nuts

Preparation Time: 5 minutes
Cooing Time: 15/20 minutes
Servings: 4
Ingredients:

- 200 g lamb chops
- 2 Tbsps. mustard
- 1 Tbsp. mixed herbs

- 1 Tbsp. breadcrumbs
- 10 g walnuts, chopped
- Salt and pepper, to taste
- 20 g breadcrumbs

Directions:

1. Pat the chops dry with paper towels.
2. Mix the walnuts, herbs, salt, pepper, and first quantity breadcrumbs together in a bowl.
3. Brush with mustard and coat each chop in the second quantity of breadcrumbs.
4. Spray a little oil in the air fryer basket.
5. Cook the chops in the air fryer preheated to 180°C for 20 minutes.
6. Serve the chops piping hot, accompanied by a side dish of your choice.

Nutrition:

Calories: 430
Carbohydrates 10 g
Fats: 15 g
Protein: 40 g

102. Lamb Chops with Lemon and Honey

Preparation Time: 5 minutes
Cooking Time: 15/20 minutes
Servings: 4

Ingredients:

- 2 lamb chops
- 2 Tbsps. honey
- 1 sprig rosemary
- 1 sprig thyme
- 20 g breadcrumbs
- 2 Tbsps. lemon juice
- Olive oil, as required
- Salt, to taste

Directions:

1. Remove the fat and any small pieces of bone from the chops. Pat them dry with paper towels.
2. Wash the rosemary and chop it finely. Do the same with the thyme sprig.
3. Put the breadcrumbs in a dish and mix with the chopped rosemary and thyme and the lemon juice.
4. Coat the chops in lemon breadcrumbs, pressing well to coat them evenly.
5. Spray the air fryer basket with cooking oil spray or an oil mister and insert the breaded chops.
6. Drizzle the chops with honey.
7. Cook them in an air fryer heated to 180ºC for 15-20 minutes, turning the ribs a couple of times and checking that they are cooked.
8. Serve the honey chops piping hot, accompanied by a sauce of your choice.

Nutrition:

Calories: 360
Carbohydrates: 6 g
Fats: 6 g
Protein: 37 g

103. Lean Lamb and Turkey Meatballs with Yogurt

Preparation Time: 10 minutes
Cooking Time: 10 minutes
Servings: 4

Ingredients:

- 1 egg white
- 4 oz. ground lean turkey
- 1 lb. lean ground lamb
- 1 tsp. each cayenne pepper, ground coriander, red chili paste, salt, and ground cumin
- 2 garlic cloves, minced
- 1 ½ Tbsp. parsley, chopped
- 1 Tbsp. mint, chopped
- ¼ cup olive oil

For the yogurt:

- 2 Tbsp. buttermilk
- 1 garlic clove, minced
- ¼ cup mint, chopped
- ½ cup Greek yogurt, non-fat
- Salt, to taste

Directions:

1. Set the Air Fryer to 390°F.
2. Blend all the ingredients for the meatballs in a bowl. Roll and mound them into golf-size round balls. Arrange in the cooking basket.
3. Cook for 8 minutes.
4. While waiting, combine all the ingredients for the mint yogurt in a bowl. Mix well.
5. Serve the meatballs with mint yogurt. Top with olives and fresh mint.

Nutrition:

Calorie: 154
Carbohydrate: 9 g
Fat: 2.5 g
Protein: 8.6 g
Fiber: 2.4 g

104. Meatballs and Creamy Potatoes

Preparation Time: 45–50 minutes
Cooking Time: 15 minutes
Servings: 4–6

Ingredients:

- 12 oz. lean ground beef
- 1 medium onion, finely chopped
- 1 Tbsp. parsley leaves, finely chopped
- ½ Tbsp. fresh thyme leaves
- ½ tsp. minced garlic

- 2 Tbsp. olive oil
- 1 tsp. salt
- 1 tsp. ground black pepper
- 1 large egg
- 3 Tbsp. bread crumbs
- 1 cup half & half, or ½ cup whole milk and ½ cup cream mixed
- 7 medium russet potatoes
- ½ tsp. ground nutmeg
- ½ cup grated Gruyere cheese

Directions:

1. Place the ground beef, onions, parsley, thyme, garlic, olive oil, salt and pepper, egg, and breadcrumbs in a bowl, and mix well. Place in refrigerator until needed.
2. In another bowl, place half & half and nutmeg, and whisk to combine.
3. Peel and wash potatoes, and then slice them thinly, 1/8- to 1/5-inch thick, or use a mandolin if needed
4. Warm up the Air Fryer to 390°F.
5. Place potato slices in a bowl with half & half and toss to coat well.
6. Layer the potato slices in an Air Fryer baking pan and pour over the leftover half & half.
7. Bake for 25 minutes at 390°F.
8. Meanwhile, take the meat mixture out of the fridge and shape it into inch and a half balls.
9. When the potatoes are cooked, place meatballs on top of them in one layer and cover with the grated Gruyere.
10. Cook for another 10 minutes.
11. Enjoy!

Nutrition:

Calories: 232
Total Fat: 8.2 g
Carbs: 6.2 g
Protein: 12.3 g

105. Pesto Coated Rack of Lamb

Preparation Time: 15 minutes
Cooking Time: 15 minutes
Servings: 4

Ingredients

- ½ bunch fresh mint
- 1 garlic clove
- ¼ cup extra-virgin olive oil
- ½ Tbsp. honey
- Salt and ground black pepper, as required
- 1 (1½ lbs.) rack of lamb

Directions:

1. For pesto: in a blender, add the mint, garlic, oil, honey, salt, and black pepper and pulse until smooth.
2. Coat the rack of lamb evenly with some pesto.
3. Set the temperature of air fryer to 200°F. Grease an air fryer basket.
4. Place rack of lamb into the prepared air fryer basket.
5. Air fry for about 15 minutes, coating with the remaining pesto after every 5 minutes.
6. Remove from air fryer and place the rack of lamb onto a cutting board for about 5 minutes to rest.
7. Cut the rack into individual chops and serve.

Nutrition:

Calories: 406
Carbohydrate: 2.9g
Protein: 34.9g
Fat: 27.7g
Sugar: 2.2g
Sodium: 161mg

106. Spiced Lamb Steaks

Preparation Time: 15 minutes
Cooking Time: 15 minutes
Servings: 3

Ingredients:

- ½ onion, roughly chopped
- 5 garlic cloves, peeled
- 1 Tbsp. fresh ginger, peeled
- 1 tsp. garam masala
- 1 tsp. ground fennel
- ½ tsp. ground cumin
- ½ tsp. ground cinnamon
- ½ tsp. cayenne pepper
- Salt and ground black pepper, as required
- 1½ lbs. boneless lamb sirloin steaks

Directions:

1. In a blender, combine the onion, garlic, ginger, and spices and pulse until smooth.
2. Transfer the mixture to a large bowl.
3. Add the lamb steaks and generously coat with the mixture.
4. Refrigerate to marinate for about 24 hours.
5. Set the temperature of air fryer to 330°F. Grease an air fryer basket.
6. Arrange steaks in the prepared air fryer basket in a single layer.
7. Air fry for about 15 minutes, flipping once halfway through.
8. Once done, remove the steaks from air fryer and serve.

Nutrition:

Calories: 252406
Carbohydrate: 4.2g
Protein: 21.7g
Fat: 16.7g
Sugar: 0.7g
Sodium: 42mg

107. Meatballs in Tomato Sauce

Preparation Time: 10 minutes
Cooking Time: 10 minutes
Servings: 3–4

Ingredients:

- 1 egg
- ¾ lb. lean ground beef
- 1 onion, chopped
- 3 Tbsp. breadcrumbs
- ½ Tbsp. fresh thyme leaves, chopped
- ½ cup tomato sauce
- 1 Tbsp. parsley, chopped
- Pinch salt
- Pinch pepper, to taste

Directions:

1. Preheat the Air Fryer to 390°F
2. Place all ingredients except the tomato sauce in a bowl. Mix until well combined. Divide mixture into 12 balls. Place them in the cooking basket.
3. Cook meatballs for 8 minutes.
4. Put the cooked meatballs in an oven dish. Pour the tomato sauce on top. Put the oven dish inside the cooking basket of the Air Fryer.
5. Cook for 5 minutes at 330°F.

Nutrition:
Calorie: 129
Carbohydrate: 15.4 g
Fat: 17.8 g
Protein: 17.6 g
Fiber: 1.2 g

108. Herbed Leg of Lamb

Preparation Time: 10 minutes
Cooking Time: 75 minutes
Servings: 3

Ingredients:

- 2 lbs. bone-in leg of lamb
- 2 Tbsps. olive oil
- Salt and ground black pepper, as required
- 2 fresh rosemary sprigs
- 2 fresh thyme sprigs

Directions:

1. Coat the leg of lamb with oil and sprinkle with salt and black pepper.
2. Wrap the leg of lamb with herb sprigs.
3. Set the temperature of air fryer to 300˚F. Grease an air fryer basket.
4. Place leg of lamb into the prepared air fryer basket.
5. Air fry for about 75 minutes.
6. Remove from air fryer and transfer the leg of lamb onto a platter.
7. With a piece of foil, cover the leg of lamb for about 10 minutes before slicing.
8. Cut the leg of lamb into desired size pieces and serve.

Nutrition:
Calories: 534
Carbohydrate: 2.4g
Protein: 69.8g
Fat: 25.8g
Sugar: 0g
Sodium: 190mg

109. Leg of Lamb with Brussels Sprout

Preparation Time: 20 minutes
Cooking Time: 90 minutes
Servings: 6

Ingredients:

- 2¼ lbs. leg of lamb
- 3 Tbsps. olive oil, divided
- 1 Tbsp. fresh rosemary, minced
- 1 Tbsp. fresh lemon thyme
- 1 garlic clove, minced
- Salt and ground black pepper, as required
- 1½ lbs. Brussels sprouts, trimmed
- 2 Tbsps. honey

Directions:

1. With a sharp knife, score the leg of lamb at several places.
2. In a bowl, mix together 2 tablespoons of oil, herbs, garlic, salt, and black pepper. Generously coat the leg of lamb with oil mixture.
3. Set the temperature of air fryer to 300˚F. Grease an air fryer basket. Place leg of lamb into the prepared air fryer basket.
4. Air fry for about 75 minutes.
5. Meanwhile, coat the Brussels sprout evenly with the remaining oil and honey.
6. Now, set the temperature of air fryer to 392˚F.
7. Arrange Brussels sprout into the air fryer basket with leg of lamb.
8. Air Fry for about 15 minutes.
9. Remove from air Fryer and transfer the leg of lamb onto a platter.
10. With a piece of foil, cover the leg of lamb for about 10 minutes before slicing.
11. Cut the leg of lamb into desired size pieces and serve alongside the Brussels sprouts.

Nutrition :
Calories : 449
Carbohydrate : 16.6g
Protein : 51.7g
Fat: 19.9g
Sugar: 8.2g
Sodium: 185mg

110. Garlic Lamb Roast

Preparation Time: 20 minutes
Cooking Time: 1½ hours
Servings: 6

Ingredients:

- 2 ¾ lbs. half lamb leg roast
- 3 garlic cloves, cut into thin slices
- 2 Tbsps. extra-virgin olive oil
- 1 Tbsp. dried rosemary, crushed
- Salt and ground black pepper, as required

Directions:

1. In a small bowl, mix together the oil, rosemary, salt, and black pepper.
2. With the tip of a sharp knife, make deep slits on the top of lamb roast fat. Insert the garlic slices into the slits.
3. Coat the lamb roast evenly with oil mixture.
4. Set the temperature of air fryer to 390°F. Grease an air fryer basket.
5. Arrange lamb in the prepared air fryer basket.
6. Air Fry for about 15 minutes and then another 1¼ hours at 320°F.
7. Remove from air fryer and transfer the roast onto a platter.
8. With a piece of foil, cover the roast for about 10 minutes before slicing.
9. Cut the roast into desired size slices and serve.

Nutrition:

Calories: 418
Carbohydrate: 0.9g
Protein: 57.4g
Fat: 14.9g
Sugar: 0g
Sodium: 165mg

111. Roast Pork Stuffed with Truffle and Mango

Preparation Time: 20 minutes
Cooking Time: 20 minutes
Servings: 4

Ingredients:

- 150 g pork loin
- 1 small mango
- 10 g truffle cream
- 20 g breadcrumbs
- 1 egg
- Olive oil, as required
- Salt and pepper, to taste

Directions:

1. Peel the mango, wash it, and remove the pit. Cut it into cubes and place it in a non-stick pan with a tablespoon of oil.
2. Cook the cubes for 5 minutes over medium heat, then switch off and place them in a bowl.
3. Put the breadcrumbs, egg, truffle, salt, and pepper in the bowl and mix until well combined.
4. Wash and dry the loin and then cut it in half horizontally. Sprinkle the inside of the meat with salt and pepper and then put the stuffing inside. Seal the meat and fasten it with kitchen string.
5. Brush the surface of the meat with olive oil, salt, and pepper it and then place it directly into the fryer basket.
6. Bake at 200°C for 10 minutes, then turn the meat and continue cooking for another 10 minutes.
7. Check loin and if the meat is still not ready, continue cooking for another 5 minutes.
8. Once done, remove the loin from the fryer and let it rest for 5 minutes.
9. Place the roast on a plate and serve.

Nutrition:

Calories: 405
Carbohydrates: 10 g
Fats: 11 g
Protein: 38 g

112. Roast pork with plums in brandy

Preparation Time: 25 minutes
Cooking Time: 20 minutes
Servings: 4

Ingredients:

- 200 g pork loin
- 2 plums
- 2 tsps. lime juice
- 40 ml. brandy
- 80 ml. vegetable broth
- Salt and pepper, to taste
- Olive oil, to taste

Directions:

1. Wash and dry the plums, cut them in half, remove the pits and place them in a bowl. Sprinkle the plums with brandy and lime juice and leave to marinate.
2. Meanwhile, tie the loin with kitchen twine.
3. Brush a pan suitable for your fryer with olive oil. Place the loin inside the baking tin and place in the air fryer for 15 minutes at 200°C.
4. After 15 minutes, take out the pan and place the plums inside, then sprinkle with the broth. Turn the roast over, place the pan back into the fryer and cook for a further 5 minutes.
5. As soon as the roast is cooked, remove it from the fryer and let it rest for 5 minutes.
6. After 5 minutes, place the roast on a serving plate. Place the plums next to the roast, sprinkle with the cooking juices and serve.

Nutrition:

Calories: 420

Carbohydrates 14 g
Fats: 12 g
Protein: 38 g

113. Pork Chops with Cherry Tomatoes and Ricotta Cheese

Preparation Time: 15 minutes
Cooking Time: 15 minutes
Servings: 4
Ingredients:

- 2 pork chops (80 g each)
- 100 g cherry tomatoes
- 2 Tbsps. chicken stock
- 1 clove garlic
- 10 g breadcrumbs
- 1 Tbsp. grated salted ricotta cheese
- 1 tsp. dried oregano
- Olive oil, as required
- Salt and pepper, to taste

Directions:

1. Wash the tomatoes under running water, dry them and then cut them in half.
2. Peel the garlic. Pat the pork chops dry with paper towels.
3. In a bowl, mix breadcrumbs, salted ricotta, oregano, a pinch of salt and pepper.
4. Place the chopped cherry tomatoes and garlic in an ovenproof dish suitable for the air fryer. Lay the chops on top.
5. Sprinkle the chops with the broth and then cover them with the breadcrumb and ricotta mixture.
6. Place the dish in the fryer basket and set the temperature to 200°C for about 15 minutes.
7. Check the chops and if not yet ready, continue for another 5 minutes.
8. Serve the chops still hot, accompanied by the cherry tomatoes and sprinkled with the cooking juices.

Nutrition :
Calories: 400
Carbohydrates: 11 g
Fats: 12 g
Protein: 39 gr

114. Pork Chops with Cream and Pink Pepper

Preparation Time: 10 minutes
Cooking Time: 30 minutes
Servings: 4
Ingredients:

- 2 small pork chops
- 1 tsp. Parmesan cheese
- 1 tsp. pink peppercorns
- Salt to, taste
- 1 tsp. chopped thyme
- 1 egg
- 30 ml heavy cream

Directions:

1. First, pat the chops dry with paper towels. Season both chops with salt and chopped thyme on both sides.
2. Now mix the Parmesan cheese, salt, and pink peppercorns in a bowl.
3. Whisk together the egg and cream in a second bowl. Dip the chops in the egg and then in the pink pepper mixture.
4. Preheat the air fryer for 2-3 minutes at 200°C and grease the basket with a little oil.
5. When the air fryer is preheated, place the chops inside it. Bake for 15-18 minutes (depending on thickness), turning halfway through.
6. Serve the chops piping hot, accompanied by your favorite sauce.

Nutrition:
Calories: 400
Carbohydrates: 9 g
Fats: 11 g
Protein: 38 g

115. Pork Chops in Barbecue Sauce and Walnuts

Preparation Time: 30 minutes
Cooking Time: 12 minutes
Servings: 4
Ingredients:

- 1 pork chop
- 2 tsps. sugar-free barbecue sauce
- 1 Tbsp. chopped walnuts
- 1 pinch garlic powder
- 1 tsp. olive oil
- Salt and pepper, to taste

Directions:

1. Let the chop rest at room temperature for about 20 minutes, then pat it dry with paper towels. Season with a little salt, pepper, and garlic powder.
2. Sprinkle the chop with 1 teaspoon of oil.
3. Place the chop on the rack and bake it at 180°C for 4 minutes.
4. After 4 minutes, brush the meat with the barbecue sauce.Continue cooking for another 4 minutes.
5. Turn the chop and brush it on the other side with barbeque sauce and sprinkle it with walnuts. Continue cooking at an increased temperature of 200°C for about 4 minutes more.
6. Once done, serve the chop directly on a serving plate with the cooking sauce.

Nutrition:
Calories: 390
Carbohydrates: 7 g

Fats: 12 g
Protein: 38 g

116. Spiced Pork Chop

Preparation Time: 15 minutes
Cooking Time: 16 minutes
Servings: 4
Ingredients:

- 1 (150 g) pork chop
- 1 clove of garlic
- 1 tsp. chopped thyme
- 1 Tbsp. meat spice mix
- Olive oil, as required
- Salt and pepper, to taste

Directions:

1. Start by peeling the garlic, then chop it finely and place it in a bowl. Add the washed and chopped thyme, the spice mix, salt, pepper and 2 teaspoons of olive oil and mix well.
2. Dry the pork chop and then coat it in the mix you have just prepared, pressing it down with your fingers so that the mixture adheres well to the meat.
3. Brush an oven dish suitable for an air fryer with olive oil and then place the chop inside.
4. Place the dish in the air fryer and bake at 180°C for 8 minutes.
5. After 8 minutes, turn the chops over and continue cooking for a further 8 minutes.
6. As soon as the pork is well cooked, remove it from the fryer and let it rest for 5 minutes.
7. Place the meat now on a plate and serve with sauce and side dish to taste.

Nutrition :
Calories: 320
Carbohydrates: 1 g
Fats: 8 g
Protein: 35 g

117. Pork Ribs with Paprika and Marjoram

Preparation Time: 5 minutes
Cooking Time: 20 minutes
Servings: 4
Ingredients:

- 3 pork ribs
- 1 pinch paprika powder
- Olive oil, as required
- Salt and pepper, to taste
- 1 Tbsp. chopped marjoram

Directions:

1. Prepare the seasoning mix with paprika, salt and marjoram and mix.
2. Dry the pork ribs with paper towels. Season the ribs with the seasoning mixture on both sides.
3. Place the ribs on the basket of the air fryer. Let them bake at 180C° for 20 minutes.
4. After 10 minutes of cooking, turn them over and continue cooking for another 10 minutes.
5. Serve the ribs hot.

Nutrition :
Calories: 350
Carbohydrates: 2 g
Fats: 10 g
Protein: 35 g

118. Spicy Pork Ribs with Pecorino Cheese

Preparation Time: 5 minutes
Cooking Time: 20 minutes
Servings: 3
Ingredients:

- 3 pork ribs
- 1 tsp. chopped red pepper
- 1 Tbsp. grated Pecorino Romano cheese
- Olive oil, as required
- Salt and pepper, to taste

Directions:

1. Mix the salt, Pecorino cheese and chopped red pepper.
2. Dry the pork ribs with paper towels. Bread the ribs with the Pecorino mix on both sides.
3. Place the ribs on the basket of the air fryer.
4. Let them bake at 180°C for 20 minutes.
5. After 10 minutes of cooking, turn them over and continue cooking for another 10 minutes.
6. Serve the ribs still hot, accompanied by a side dish of your choice.

Nutrition :
Calories: 365
Carbohydrates: 2 g
Fats: 12 g
Protein: 36 g

119. Spicy Pork Cutlets

Preparation Time: 10 minutes
Cooking Time: 10 minutes
Servings: 4
Ingredients:

- 150 g pork loin
- 2 small eggs
- 1 pinch salt
- 1 tsp. meat spice mix
- 30 g breadcrumbs
- Olive oil, as required
- Salt and pepper, to taste

Directions:

1. Break two whole eggs in a dish with a pinch of salt and beat them with a fork. Cut the pork loin into 1-inch thick slices.
2. In another dish, put the breadcrumbs and mix with salt, pepper, and spice mix.
3. Dip and bread the slices of meat (one at a time) first in egg, then in breadcrumbs, coating them thoroughly on both sides.
4. Spray the breaded slices well with cooking oil spray. Place the cutlets into the basket of the air fryer.
5. Bake at 180°C for about 10 minutes.
6. When done, serve the cutlets with a side dish to taste.

Nutrition :
Calories: 330
Carbohydrates: 8 g
Fats: 7 g
Protein: 34 g

120. Pork Cubes with Turmeric, Ginger, and Walnuts

Preparatiion Time: 10 minutes
Cooking Time: 15 minutes
Servings: 4
Ingredients:

- 200 g pork loin
- 10 g chopped walnuts
- 10 ml soy sauce
- 10 g fresh ginger
- 1 tsp. turmeric
- ½ shallot
- 1 clove garlic
- Flour, as required
- Salt and pepper, to taste
- Oil, to taste

Directions:

1. First, dry the pork loin with paper towels, remove any excess skin or fat, and then cut it into large cubes. Dredge them in flour and set them aside.
2. Peel the shallot and chop it. Peel the garlic and chop it. Peel and grate the ginger. Put a tablespoon of olive oil in the bottom of an oven dish suitable for the air fryer together with the shallots and garlic. Add the ginger and pork loin.
3. Pour in the soy sauce and two tablespoons of water.
4. Sprinkle with the walnuts and turmeric and cook in the air fryer preheated to 200°C for about 15 minutes.
5. When the pork loin is ready, remove it from the air fryer and serve it immediately sprinkled with the cooking juices.

Nutrition:
Calories: 480
Carbohydrates: 7 g
Fats: 27 g
Protein: 38 g

121. Pork Fillet with Almonds and Brandy

Preparation Time: 20 minutes
Cooking Time: 16 minutes
Servings: 4
Ingredients:

- 150 g pork fillet
- 1 Tbsp. chopped almonds
- 60 ml brandy
- 1 celery stalk
- 1 small spring onion
- 1 sprig thyme
- Olive oil, as required
- Salt and pepper, to taste

Directions:

1. First, clean, wash and dry the spring onion, then chop it finely. Remove the end and white filaments from the celery, and chop it.
2. Dry the pork fillet and season the meat on both sides with salt and pepper.
3. Take a pan suitable for the air fryer and place the chopped spring onion and celery inside. Add 2 teaspoons of olive oil and the pork and transfer the pan to the air fryer.
4. Cook the fillet at 200°C for 3 minutes, then deglaze with brandy.
5. Cook for 5 minutes, then remove the celery and spring onion from the pork fillet.
6. For the sauce, place the thyme leaves, spring onion, celery and chopped almonds in a blender and blend with a little brandy.
7. Sprinkle the fillet with the mixture and put it back into the air fryer for another 8 minutes.
8. Check the prok chop, and if it is not done, continue cooking for another 2 minutes.
9. Slice the pork fillet and serve it sprinkled with the cooking juices.

Nutrition :
Calories: 370
Carbohydrates: 7 g
Fats: 6 g
Protein: 36 g

122.Pork Loin with Hazelnuts and Mustard

Preparation Time: 20 minutes
Cooking Time: 15 minutes
Servings: 4
Ingredients:

- 150 g pork fillet
- 1 Tbsp. chopped hazelnuts
- 1 tsp. paprika
- 2 Tbsps. breadcrumbs
- 2 eggs
- 2 tsps. mustard
- 2 tsps. honey
- Olive oil, as required
- Salt and pepper, to taste

Directions:

1. Pat dry the pork fillet, removing any excess fat.
2. Put the breadcrumbs and paprika in a deep dish and mix them together with the nuts.
3. Whisk together the eggs and olive oil in another bowl.
4. Mix mustard with honey and 1 teaspoon olive oil in a dish. Brush the surface of the pork fillet with the mustard mixture.
5. Dredge the mustard pork fillet in the egg mixture and then in the nut mixture, shaking to remove the excess. Place the fillet inside an oven dish suitable for an air fryer.
6. Bake at 190°C for about 15 minutes.
7. Check to see if the fillet is done, and continue cooking for another 5 minutes if needed.
8. Serve your pork fillet with your favorite sauce and a side dish of your choice.

Nutrition:
Calories: 390
Carbohydrates: 11 g
Fats: 6 g
Protein: 36 g

123. Pork Fillet with Peas and Carrots

Preparation Time: 20-30 minutes
Cooking Time: 10-15 minutes
Servings: 4
Ingredients:

- 150 g pork fillet
- 1 Tbsp. white wine
- 80 g canned peas
- ½ carrot
- Sage, to taste
- Thyme, to taste
- Olive oil, as required
- Salt, to taste

Directions:

1. Dry and salt the pork fillet. Drain the peas and wash the half carrot. Cut the carrot into cubes.
2. Chop both sage and thyme. Place the pork fillet with the vegetables in a pan suitable for your air fryer.
3. Pour over the white wine, chopped herbs, and bake at 200°C for 10-15 minutes, shaking the basket from time to time.
4. Serve the pork fillet accompanied by the vegetables.

Nutrition :
Calories: 470
Carbohydrates: 16 g
Fats: 6 g
Protein: 40 g

124.Pork Fillet with Pistachio Rum and Green Pepper Sauce

Preparation Time: 20 minutes
Cooking Time: 15 minutes
Servings: 4
Ingredients:

- 100 g whole pork fillet
- 15 g pistachio flour
- 1 tsp. green peppercorns
- 40 ml fresh cream
- 20 ml rum
- 1 clove garlic
- Salt and pepper, to taste
- Olive oil, to taste

Directions:

1. First, peel and mince the garlic.
2. Remove the excess fat from the pork fillet and then dry it with kitchen paper towels. Rub the entire surface of the meat with garlic, then brush it with oil, and season with salt and pepper.
3. Place the fillet into the basket of the air fryer and cook at 180°C for 15 minutes.
4. Turn and brush the meat with oil after 10 minutes.
5. As soon as it is cooked, remove it from the air fryer and let it rest for 5 minutes.
6. Meanwhile, prepare the pistachio, rum, and green pepper sauce: Put a tablespoon of olive oil in a frying pan and once hot enough, add the pistachio flour. Brown for 2 minutes, then add the rum.
7. Stir in the wine and then add the cream and green peppercorns. Let the sauce thicken, adjust salt, and pepper and switch off.
8. Cut the fillet into thin slices.
9. Place the pork slices on a plate, sprinkle the entire surface of the meat with the sauce and serve

Nutrition :
Calories: 280

Carbohydrates: 3 g
Fats: 12 g
Protein: 29 g

125.Beef Korma Curry

Preparation Time: 10 minutes
Cooking Time: 17–20 minutes
Servings: 4

Ingredients:

- 1 lb. (454 g) sirloin steak, sliced
- ½ cup yogurt
- 1 Tbsp. curry powder
- 1 Tbsp. olive oil
- 1 onion, chopped
- 2 cloves garlic, minced
- 1 tomato, diced
- ½ cup frozen baby peas, thawed

Directions:

1. In a medium bowl, combine the steak, yogurt, and curry powder. Stir and set aside.
2. In air fryer pan, combine the olive oil, onion, and garlic. Bake at 350°F (177°C) for 3 to 4 minutes or until crisp and tender.
3. Add the steak along with the yogurt and the diced tomato. Bake for 12 -13 minutes or until the steak is almost tender.
4. Stir in the peas and bake for 2 to 3 minutes or until hot.

Nutrition:
Calories: 299
Fat: 11 g
Protein: 38 g
Carbs: 9 g
Fiber: 2 g
Sugar: 3 g
Sodium: 100 mg

126.Beef Fried Steak

Preparation Time: 15 minutes
Cooking Time: 12–16 minutes
Servings: 4

Ingredients:

- 4 (6 oz.) beef cube steaks
- ½ cup buttermilk
- 1 cup flour
- 2 tsp. paprika
- 1 tsp. garlic salt
- 1 egg
- 1 cup soft bread crumbs
- 2 Tbsp. olive oil

Directions:

1. Place the cube steaks on a plate or cutting board and gently pound until they are slightly thinner. Set aside.
2. In a shallow bowl, combine the buttermilk, flour, paprika, garlic salt, and egg until combined.
3. On a plate, combine the bread crumbs and olive oil and mix well.
4. Dip the steaks into the buttermilk batter to coat and let sit on a plate for 5 minutes.
5. Dredge the steaks in the bread crumbs. Pat the crumbs onto both sides to coat the steaks thoroughly.
6. Air fry the steaks at 350°F (177°C) for 12 to 16 minutes or until the meat reaches 160°F (71°C) on a meat thermometer and the coating is brown and crisp. You can serve this with heated beef gravy.

Nutrition:
Calories: 631
Fat: 21 g
Protein: 61 g
Carbs: 46 g
Fiber: 2 g
Sugar: 3 g
Sodium: 358 mg

127.Lemon Greek Beef and Vegetables

Preparation Time: 10 minutes
Cooking Time: 9–19 minutes
Servings: 4

Ingredients:

- ½ lb. (227 g) 96% lean ground beef
- 2 medium tomatoes, chopped
- 1 onion, chopped
- 2 garlic cloves, minced
- 2 cups. fresh baby spinach
- 2 Tbsp. freshly squeezed lemon juice
- 1/3 cup low-sodium beef broth
- 2 Tbsp. crumbled low-sodium feta cheese

Directions:

1. In a baking pan, crumble the beef. Place it in the air fryer basket. Air fry at 370°F (188°C) for 3-7 minutes, stirring once during cooking until browned. Drain off any fat or liquid.
2. Place the tomatoes, onion, and garlic into the pan. Air fry for 4-8 minutes more, or until the onion is tender.
3. Add the spinach, lemon juice, and beef broth.
4. Air fry for 2-4 minutes more, or until the spinach is wilted.
5. Sprinkle with the feta cheese and serve immediately.

Nutrition:
Calories: 98
Fat: 1 g
Protein: 15 g
Carbs: 5 g
Fiber: 1 g
Sugar: 2 g
Sodium: 123 mg

128. Country-Style Pork Ribs

Preparation Time: 5 minutes
Cooking Time: 20–25 minutes
Servings: 4

Ingredients:

- 12 country-style pork ribs, trimmed of excess fat
- 2 Tbsp. cornstarch
- 2 Tbsp. olive oil
- 1 tsp. dry mustard
- ½ tsp. thyme
- ½ tsp. garlic powder
- 1 tsp. dried marjoram
- Pinch of salt
- Freshly ground black pepper, to taste

Directions:

1. Place the ribs on a clean work surface.
2. In a small bowl, combine the cornstarch, olive oil, mustard, thyme, garlic powder, marjoram, salt, and pepper, and rub into the ribs.
3. Place the ribs in the air fryer basket and roast at 400°F (204°C) for 10 minutes.
4. Carefully turn the ribs using tongs and roast for 10 to 15 minutes or until the ribs are crisp and register an internal temperature of at least 150°F (66°C).

Nutrition:
Calories: 579
Fat: 44 g
Protein: 40 g
Carbs: 4 g
Fiber: 0 g
Sugar: 0 g
Sodium: 155 mg

129. Lemon and Honey Pork Tenderloin

Preparation Time: 5 minutes
Cooking Time: 10 minutes
Servings: 4

Ingredients:

- 1 (1 lb./454 g) pork tenderloin, cut into ½-inch slices
- 1 Tbsp. olive oil
- 1 Tbsp. freshly squeezed lemon juice
- 1 Tbsp. honey
- ½ tsp. grated lemon zest
- ½ tsp. dried marjoram
- Pinch salt
- Freshly ground black pepper, to taste

Directions:

1. Put the pork tenderloin slices in a medium bowl.
2. In another bowl, combine the olive oil, lemon juice, honey, lemon zest, marjoram, salt, and pepper. Mix.
3. Pour this marinade over the tenderloin slices and massage gently with your hand to work it into the pork.
4. Place the pork in the air fryer basket and roast at 400°F (204°C) for 10 minutes or until the pork registers at least 145°F (63°C) using a meat thermometer.

Nutrition:
Calories: 208
Fat: 8 g
Protein: 30 g
Carbs: 5 g
Fiber: 0 g
Sugar: 4
Sodium: 104 mg

130. Dijon Pork Tenderloin

Preparation Time: 10 minutes
Cooking Time: 12–14 minutes
Servings: 4

Ingredients:

- 1 lb. (454 g) pork tenderloin, cut into 1-inch slices
- Pinch salt
- Freshly ground black pepper, to taste
- 2 Tbsp. Dijon mustard
- 1 clove garlic, minced
- ½ tsp. dried basil
- 1 cup soft bread crumbs
- 2 Tbsp. olive oil

Directions:

1. Slightly pound the pork slices until they are about ¾-inch thick. Sprinkle with salt and pepper on both sides.
2. Coat the pork with the Dijon mustard and sprinkle with the garlic and basil.
3. On a plate, combine the bread crumbs and olive oil and mix well. Coat the pork slices with the bread crumb mixture, patting, so the crumbs adhere.
4. Place the pork in the air fryer basket, leaving a little space between each piece. Air fry at 390°F (199°C) for 12 to 14 minutes or until the pork reaches at least 145°F (63°C) on a meat thermometer and the coating is crisp and brown. Serve immediately.

Nutrition:
Calories: 336
Fat: 13 g
Protein: 34 g
Carbs: 20 g
Fiber: 2 g
Sugar 2 g
Sodium: 390 mg

131. Air Fryer Pork Satay

Preparation Time: 15 minutes
Cooking Time: 9–14 minutes
Servings: 4

Ingredients:

- 1 (1 lb./454 g) pork tenderloin, cut into 1½-inch cubes
- ¼ cup minced onion
- 2 garlic cloves, minced
- 1 jalapeño pepper, minced
- 2 Tbsp. freshly squeezed lime juice
- 2 Tbsp. coconut milk
- 2 Tbsp. unsalted peanut butter
- 2 tsp. curry powder

Directions:

1. In a medium bowl, mix the pork, onion, garlic, jalapeño, lime juice, coconut milk, peanut butter, and curry powder until well combined. Let it marinate for 10 minutes at room temperature.
2. With a slotted spoon, remove the pork from the marinade. Reserve the marinade.
3. Thread the pork onto about 8 bamboo or metal skewers. Air fry at 380°F (193°C) for 9-14 minutes, brushing once with the reserved marinade until the pork reaches at least 145°F (63°C) on a meat thermometer. Discard any remaining marinade. Serve immediately.

Nutrition:
Calories: 195
Fat: 7 g
Protein: 25 g
Carbs: 7 g
Fiber: 1 g
Sugar: 3 g
Sodium: 65 mg

132. Pork Burgers with Red Cabbage Slaw

Preparation Time: 20 minutes
Cooking Time: 7–9 minutes
Servings: 4

Ingredients:

- ½ cup Greek yogurt
- 2 Tbsp. low-sodium mustard, divided
- 1 Tbsp. freshly squeezed lemon juice
- ¼ cup sliced red cabbage
- ¼ cup grated carrots
- 1 lb. (454 g) lean ground pork
- ½ tsp. paprika
- 1 cup mixed baby lettuce greens
- 2 small tomatoes, sliced
- 8 small low-sodium whole-wheat sandwich buns, cut in half

Directions:

1. In a small bowl, mix the yogurt, 1 Tbsp. mustard, lemon juice, cabbage, and carrots; mix and refrigerate.
2. In a medium bowl, combine the pork, remaining 1 Tbsp. mustard, and paprika. Form 8 small patties.
3. Lay the patties into the air fryer basket. Air fry at 400°F (204°C) for 7-9 minutes, or until the patties register 165°F (74°C) as tested with a meat thermometer.
4. Assemble the burgers by placing some of the lettuce greens on the bun bottom. Top with a tomato slice, the patties, and the cabbage mixture. Add the bun on top and serve immediately.

Nutrition:
Calories: 473
Fat: 15 g
Protein: 35 g
Carbs: 51 g
Fiber: 8 g
Sugar: 8 g
Sodium: 138 mg

133. Greek Lamb Pita Pockets

Preparation Time: 15 minutes
Cooking Time: 5–7 minutes
Servings: 4

Ingredients:
Dressing:

- 1 cup plain Greek yogurt
- 1 Tbsp. lemon juice
- 1 tsp dried dill weed, crushed
- 1 tsp. ground oregano
- ½ tsp. salt

Meatballs:

- ½ lb. (227 g) ground lamb
- 1 Tbsp. diced onion
- 1 tsp. dried parsley
- 1 tsp. dried dill weed, crushed
- ¼ tsp. oregano
- ¼ tsp. coriander
- ¼ tsp. ground cumin
- ¼ tsp. salt

- 4 pita halves

Suggested Toppings:

- Red onion, slivered
- Seedless cucumber, thinly sliced
- Crumbled feta cheese
- Sliced black olives
- Chopped fresh peppers

Directions:

1. Stir dressing ingredients together and refrigerate while preparing lamb.
2. Combine all meatball ingredients in a large bowl and stir to distribute seasonings.
3. Shape the meat mixture into 12 small meatballs, rounded or slightly flattened if you prefer.
4. Air fry at 390°F (199°C) for 5-7 minutes, until well done. Remove and drain on paper towels.
5. To serve, pile meatballs and your choice of toppings in pita pockets and drizzle with dressing.

Nutrition:
Calories: 270
Fat: 14 g
Protein: 18 g
Carbs: 18 g
Fiber: 2 g
Sugar: 2 g
Sodium: 618 mg

134. Rosemary Lamb Chops

Preparation Time: 30 minutes
Cooking Time: 20 minutes
Servings: 2 to 3

Ingredients:

- 2 tsp. oil
- ½ tsp. ground rosemary
- ½ tsp. lemon juice
- 1 lb. (454 g) lamb chops, approximately 1-inch thick
- Salt and pepper, to taste
- Cooking spray

Directions:

1. Mix the oil, rosemary, and lemon juice, and rub into all sides of the lamb chops. Season to taste with salt and pepper.
2. For best flavor, cover lamb chops and allow them to rest in the fridge for 15 to 20 minutes.
3. Spray air fryer basket with nonstick spray and place lamb chops in it.
4. Air fry at 360°F (182°C) for approximately 20 minutes. This will cook chops to medium. The meat will be juicy but have no remaining pink. Air fry for 1 to 2 minutes longer for well-done chops. For rare chops, stop cooking after about 12 minutes and check for doneness.

Nutrition:
Calories: 237
Fat: 13 g
Protein: 30 g
Carbs: 0 g
Fiber: 0 g
Sugar 0 g
Sodium: 116 mg

135. Delicious Meatballs

Preparation Time: 15 Minutes
Cooking Time: 25 Minutes
Servings: 6

Ingredients:

- 200 g ground beef
- 200 g ground chicken
- 100 g ground pork
- 30 g minced garlic
- 1 potato
- 1 egg
- 1 tsp. basil
- 1 tsp. cayenne pepper
- 1 tsp. white pepper
- 2 tsp. olive oil

Directions:

1. Combine ground beef, chicken meat, and pork in the mixing bowl, and stir it gently.
2. Sprinkle it with basil, cayenne pepper, and white pepper. Add minced garlic and egg.
3. Stir the mixture gently. You should get a fluffy mass.
4. Peel the potato and grate it. Add grated potato to the mixture and stir it again.
5. Preheat the air fryer oven to 180°C.
6. Take a tray and spray it with olive oil.
7. Make the balls from the meat mixture and put them on the tray.
8. Place the tray in the oven and cook for 25 minutes.

Nutrition:
Calories: 204
Proteins: 26.0 g
Fats: 7.6 g
Carbohydrates: 7.1 g

136. Low-fat Steak

Preparation Time: 25 Minutes
Cooking Time: 10 Minutes
Servings: 3

Ingredients:

- 400 g beef steak
- 1 tsp. white pepper
- 1 tsp. turmeric

- 1 tsp. cilantro
- 1 tsp. olive oil
- 3 tsp. lemon juice
- 1 tsp. oregano
- 1 tsp. salt
- 100 ml water

Directions:

1. Rub the steaks with white pepper and turmeric, and put them in a large bowl.
2. Sprinkle the meat with salt, oregano, cilantro, and lemon juice. Leave the steaks for 20 minutes.
3. Preheat the air fryer oven to 360°C.
4. Combine olive oil and water, and pour it into an air fryer pan with steaks.
5. Grill the steaks in the air fryer for 10 minutes on both sides.
6. Serve immediately.

Nutrition:
Calories: 268
Proteins: 40.7 g
Fats: 10.1 g
Carbohydrates: 1.4 g

137.Diet Boiled Ribs

Preparation Time: 10 Minutes
Cooking Time: 30 Minutes
Servings: 4

Ingredients:

- 400 g pork ribs
- 1 tsp. black pepper
- 1 g bay leaf
- 1 tsp. basil
- 1 white onion
- 1 carrot
- 1 tsp. cumin
- 700 ml water

Directions:

1. Preheat the air fryer oven to 320°C.
2. Cut the ribs into portions and sprinkle them with black pepper.
3. Take a big air fryer pan and pour the water into it. Add the ribs and bay leaf.
4. Peel the onion and carrot, and add them to the water with the meat. Sprinkle with cumin and basil.
5. Cook at 320°C in the air fryer for 30 minutes.

Nutrition:
Calories: 294
Proteins: 27.1 g
Fats: 17.9 g
Carbohydrates: 4.8 g

138.Meatloaf

Preparation Time: 15 Minutes
Cooking Time: 30 Minutes
Servings: 4

Ingredients:

- 300 g ground beef
- 1 egg
- 1 onion
- 100 g carrot
- 1 tsp. black pepper
- 1 tsp. chili pepper
- 2 tsp. olive oil

Directions:

1. Take the ground beef and put it in a large bowl. Add egg, black pepper, and chili pepper. Stir the mixture gently.
2. Peel the carrot and onion, and chop them.
3. Add the chopped carrot and onion to the bowl with meat and stir gently.
4. Preheat the air fryer to 200°C.
5. Take the tray and spray it inside with olive oil. Make a loaf from the meat and put it on the tray.
6. Place the tray in the oven and cook for 30 minutes.

Nutrition:
Calories: 198
Proteins: 24.7 g
Fats: 8.1 g
Carbohydrates: 5.6 g

139.Beef with Mushrooms

Preparation Time: 15 Minutes
Cooking Time: 40 Minutes
Servings: 4

Ingredients:

- 300 g beef roast
- 150 g mushrooms
- 1 onion
- 1 tsp. olive oil
- 100 g vegetable broth
- 1 tsp. basil
- 1 tsp. chili
- 30 g tomato juice

Directions:

1. Take the beef and pierce it several times with a knife. Rub with olive oil, basil, chili, and lemon juice.
2. Chop the onion and mushrooms, and soak them with vegetable broth.
3. Take a big tray and put the meat in it. Add vegetable broth and vegetables to the tray.

4. Preheat the air fryer oven to 180°C and cook for 35 minutes.

Nutrition:
Calories: 175
Proteins: 24.9 g
Fats: 6.2 g
Carbohydrates: 4.4 g

140. Quick and Juicy Pork Chops

Preparation Time: 10 minutes
Cooking Time: 12 minutes
Servings: 4

Ingredients:

- 4 pork chops
- 1 tsp. olive oil
- 1 tsp. onion powder
- 1 tsp. paprika
- Pepper
- Salt

Directions:

1. Cover pork chops with olive oil and season with paprika, onion powder, pepper, and salt.
2. Place the tray in the air fryer.
3. Place pork chops on the tray.
4. Close the air fryer with the air fryer lid, select air fry mode, and then set the temperature to 380°F and timer for 12 minutes. Turn pork chops halfway through.
5. Serve and enjoy.

Nutrition:
Calories: 270
Fat: 21.1 g
Carbohydrates: 0.8 g
Sugar: 0.3 g
Protein: 18.1 g
Cholesterol: 69 mg

141. Delicious and Tender Pork Chops

Preparation Time: 10 minutes
Cooking Time: 12 minutes
Servings: 2

Ingredients:

- 2 pork chops
- 1 Tbsp. olive oil
- ¼ tsp. garlic powder
- ½ tsp. onion powder
- 1 tsp. ground mustard
- 1 ½ tsp. pepper
- 1 Tbsp. paprika
- 2 Tbsp. brown sugar
- 1 ½ tsp. salt

Directions:

1. In a small bowl, mix garlic powder, onion powder, mustard, paprika, pepper, brown sugar, and salt.
2. Cover pork chops with olive oil and rub with spice mixture.
3. Place the baking tray in the air fryer basket.
4. Place pork chops on the tray.
5. Close the air fryer, select air fry mode, and then set the temperature to 400°F and timer for 12 minutes. Turn pork chops halfway through.
6. Serve and enjoy.

Nutrition:
Calories: 375
Fat: 27.9 g
Carbohydrates: 13.1 g
Sugar: 9.5 g
Protein: 19.2 g
Cholesterol: 69 mg

142. Perfect Pork Chops

Preparation Time: 10 minutes
Cooking Time: 15 minutes
Servings: 4

Ingredients:

- 4 pork chops
- Pepper
- Salt

Directions:

1. Season pork chops with pepper and salt.
2. Place the air fryer tray in the air fryer basket.
3. Place pork chops on the tray.
4. Close the air fryer, select air fry mode, and then set the temperature to 400°F and timer for 15 minutes. Turn pork chops halfway through.
5. Serve and enjoy.

Nutrition:
Calories: 256
Fat: 19.9 g
Carbohydrates: 0 g
Sugar: 0 g
Protein: 18 g
Cholesterol: 69 mg

143. Herb Butter Lamb Chops

Preparation Time: 10 minutes
Cooking Time: 10 minutes
Servings: 4

Ingredients:

- 4 lamb chops
- 1 tsp. rosemary, chopped
- 1 Tbsp. butter
- Pepper
- Salt

Directions:

1. Season lamb chops with pepper and salt.
2. Place the air fryer tray in the air fryer basket.
3. Place lamb chops on the tray.
4. Close the air fryer, select air fry mode, and then set the temperature to 400°F and timer for 10 minutes.
5. Mix butter and rosemary, and spread on overcooked lamb chops.
6. Serve and enjoy.

Nutrition:

Calories: 278
Fat: 12.8 g
Carbohydrates: 0.2 g
Sugar: 0 g
Protein: 38 g
Cholesterol: 129 mg

144.Za'atar Lamb Chops

Preparation Time: 10 minutes
Cooking Time: 10 minutes
Servings: 4

Ingredients:

- 4 lamb loin chops
- ½ Tbsp. Za'atar seasoning
- 1 Tbsp. fresh lemon juice
- 1 tsp. olive oil
- 2 garlic cloves, minced
- Pepper
- Salt

Directions:

1. Coat lamb chops with oil and lemon juice, and rub with Za'atar, garlic, pepper, and salt.
2. Place the air fryer tray in the air fryer basket.
3. Place lamb chops on the tray.
4. Close the air fryer, select air fry mode, and then set the temperature to 400°F and timer for 10 minutes. Turn lamb chops halfway through.
5. Serve and enjoy.

Nutrition:

Calories: 266
Fat: 11.2 g
Carbohydrates: 0.6 g
Sugar: 0.1 g
Protein: 38 g
Cholesterol: 122 mg

Chapter 6. Poultry Recipes

N. 149 Stuffed Chicken
N. 153 Chicken Casserole
N. 157 Chicken Tikka Kebab
N. 169 Tender Chicken Teriyaki
N. 175 Duck Breast with Figs
N. 183 Gyro Seasoned Chicken

145. Warm Chicken and Spinach Salad

Preparation Time: 10 Minutes
Cooking Time: 16 to 20 Minutes
Servings: 4

Ingredients:

- 3 (5 oz.) boneless, skinless chicken breasts, cut into 1-inch cubes
- 5 tsp. olive oil
- ½ tsp. dried thyme
- 1 medium red onion, sliced
- 1 red bell pepper, sliced
- 1 small zucchini, cut into strips
- 3 Tbsp. freshly squeezed lemon juice
- 6 cups fresh baby spinach

Directions:

1. Preheat the air fryer to 260°C.
2. In a bowl, blend the chicken with olive oil and thyme. Toss to coat. Transfer to an air fryer pan and roast for 8 minutes in the air fryer.
3. Add the red onion, red bell pepper, and zucchini. Roast for 8-12 minutes more, stirring once during cooking, or until the chicken reaches an inner temperature of 165°F on a meat thermometer.
4. Remove the pan from the air fryer and stir in the lemon juice.
5. Lay the spinach in a serving bowl and top with the chicken mixture. Toss to combine and serve immediately.

Nutrition:
Calories: 214
Fat: 7 g (29% of calories from fat)
Saturated Fat: 1 g
Protein: 28 g
Carbohydrates: 7 g
Sodium: 116 mg
Fiber: 2 g
Sugar 4 g

146. Chicken in Tomato Juice

Preparation Time: 20 Minutes
Cooking Time: 15 Minutes
Servings: 3

Ingredients:

- 350 g chicken breast fillet
- 200 g tomato juice
- 100 g tomatoes
- 2 tsp. basil
- 1 tsp. chili
- 1 tsp. oregano
- 1 tsp. rosemary
- 1 tsp. olive oil
- 1 tsp. mint
- 1 tsp. lemon juice

Directions:

1. Make the tomato sauce: combine basil, chili, oregano, rosemary, olive oil, mint, and lemon juice, and stir the mixture.
2. Use an immersion blender to blend the mixture until smooth.
3. Take a chicken fillet and separate it into three portions. Put the meat in the tomato mixture and leave for 15 minutes.
4. Meanwhile, preheat the air fryer oven to 230°C.
5. Put the meat mixture on the tray and bake it in the oven for at least 15 minutes.

Nutrition:
Calories: 258
Proteins: 34.8 g
Fats: 10.5 g
Carbohydrates: 5.0 g

147. Chicken Wings with Curry

Preparation Time: 15 Minutes
Cooking Time: 20 Minutes
Servings: 4

Ingredients:

- 400 g chicken wings
- 30 g curry
- 1 tsp. chili
- 1 tsp. cayenne pepper
- 1 tsp. salt
- 1 lemon, juiced
- 1 tsp. basil
- 1 tsp. oregano
- 3 tsp. mustard
- 1 tsp. olive oil

Directions:

1. Rub the wings with chili, curry, cayenne pepper, salt, basil, and oregano. Transfer to a bowl and let the mixture sit for at least 10 minutes in the fridge.
2. Take the mixture from the fridge and add mustard, and sprinkle with lemon juice. Stir the mix gently again.
3. Spray the pan with olive oil and put the wings in it.
4. Preheat the air fryer oven to 180°C and put wings inside.
5. Cook for 20 minutes.

Nutrition:
Calories: 244
Proteins: 30.8 g
Fats: 10.6 g
Carbohydrates: 7.2 g

148. Chicken Meatballs

Preparation Time: 15 Minutes
Cooking Time: 20 Minutes
Servings: 6

Ingredients:

- 400 g ground chicken
- 100 g chopped dill
- 2 tsp. olive oil
- 100 ml tomato juice
- 1 tsp. black pepper
- 1 tsp. white pepper
- 1 egg
- 20 ml milk

Directions:

1. Put the ground chicken in a mixing bowl. Add chopped dill, black and white pepper, and mix gently.
2. Add egg and mix again.
3. Make balls from the mixture and make the sauce from tomato juice and milk.
4. Pour the sauce into the air fryer tray and add the meatballs to it.
5. Preheat the air fryer oven to 180°C and put the meatballs in it.
6. Cook for 20 minutes and serve immediately.

Nutrition:
Calories: 199
Proteins: 23.9 g
Fats: 8.1 g
Carbohydrates: 10.7 g

149. Stuffed Chicken

Preparation Time: 15 Minutes
Cooking Time: 30 Minutes
Servings: 4

Ingredients:

- 2 chicken breasts
- 2 tomatoes
- 200 g basil
- 1 tsp. black pepper
- 1 tsp. cayenne pepper
- 100 ml tomato juice
- 40 g goat cheese

Directions:

1. Cut the chicken breast partly in half lengthwise to form a "pocket" and rub it with black pepper and cayenne pepper.
2. Slice tomatoes and chop basil. Chop the goat cheese.
3. Combine all the ingredients except the chicken and tomato juice.
4. Fill the chicken breasts with this mixture.
5. If needed, use several toothpicks to close the pocket.
6. Preheat the air fryer oven to 200°C. Put the chicken breasts in the tray and pour the tomato juice over it.
7. Cook the chicken breasts for 30 minutes. Serve.

Nutrition:
Calories: 312
Proteins: 41.6 g
Fats: 13.4 g
Carbohydrates: 5.6 g

150. Duo Crisp Chicken Wings

Preparation Time: 10 minutes
Cooking Time: 18 minutes
Servings: 6

Ingredients:

- 12 chicken wings
- 1/2 cup chicken broth
- Salt and black pepper, to taste
- 1/4 cup melted butter

Directions:

1. Set a metal rack in the Instant Pot Duo Crisp and pour broth into it.
2. Place the wings on the metal rack, then put on its pressure-cooking lid.
3. Hit the "Pressure Button" and select 8 minutes of cooking time, then press "Start."
4. Once the Instant Pot Duo beeps, do a quick release and remove its lid.
5. Transfer the pressure-cooked wings to a plate.
6. Empty the pot and set an Air Fryer Basket in the Instant Pot Duo
7. Toss the wings with butter and seasoning.
8. Spread the seasoned wings in the Air Fryer Basket.
9. Put on the Air Fryer lid, press the Air fryer Button, and then set the time to 10 minutes.
10. Once done, remove the lid and serve.

Nutrition:
Calories: 246
Total Fat: 18.9 g
Saturated Fat: 7 g
Cholesterol: 115 mg
Sodium: 149 mg
Total Carbohydrate: 0 g
Dietary Fiber: 0 g
Total Sugars: 0 g
Protein: 20.2 g

151. Italian Whole Chicken

Preparation Time: 10 minutes
Cooking Time: 35 minutes
Servings: 4

Ingredients:

- 1 whole chicken
- 2 Tbsp. spray oil of choice
- 1 tsp. garlic powder
- 1 tsp. onion powder
- 1 tsp. paprika
- 1 tsp. Italian seasoning
- 2 Tbsp. Montreal steak seasoning
- 1 ½ cup chicken broth

Directions:

1. Whisk all the seasoning in a bowl and rub it on the chicken.
2. Set a metal rack in the Instant Pot Duo Crisp and pour broth into it.
3. Place the chicken on the metal rack, then put on its pressure-cooking lid.
4. Press the "Pressure Button" and select 25 minutes of cooking time, then press "Start."
5. Once the Instant Pot Duo beeps, do a natural release and remove its lid.
6. Transfer the pressure-cooked chicken to a plate.
7. Empty the pot and set an Air Fryer Basket in the Instant Pot Duo.
8. Toss the chicken pieces with oil to coat well.
9. Spread the seasoned chicken in the air Fryer Basket.
10. Put on the Air Fryer lid, press the Air fryer Button, and then set the time to 10 minutes.
11. Remove the lid and serve.
12. For a standard air fryer, place the chicken that is rubbed with oil and the spice mix in a pre-heated air fryer at 250°C and bake for 25 minutes or until done.
13. Enjoy!

Nutrition:
Calories: 163
Total Fat: 10.7 g
Saturated Fat: 2 g
Cholesterol: 33 mg
Sodium: 1439 mg
Total Carbohydrate: 1.8 g
Dietary Fiber: 0.3 g
Total Sugars: 0.8 g
Protein: 12.6 g

152. Chicken Vegetable Stew

Preparation Time: 10 minutes
Cooking Time: 17 minutes
Servings: 6

Ingredients:

- 2 Tbsp. olive oil
- 1 lb. chicken breast, cubed
- 1 Tbsp. garlic powder
- 1 Tbsp. thyme
- 1 Tbsp. pepper
- 1 cup chicken broth
- 12 oz. bag frozen mixed vegetables
- 4 large potatoes, peeled and cut into 2cm. cubes
- 10 oz. can cream of chicken soup
- 1 cup heavy cream

Directions:

1. Press Sauté on the Instant Pot Duo Crisp and add the chicken and olive oil.
2. Sauté the chicken for 5 minutes, then stir in spices.
3. Pour in the broth along with vegetables and cream of chicken soup.
4. Put on the pressure-cooking lid and seal it.
5. Hit the "Pressure Button" and select 10 minutes of cooking time, then press "Start."
6. Once the Instant Pot Duo beeps, do a quick release and remove its lid.
7. Remove the lid and stir in cream.
8. Press the sauté button and cook for 2 minutes.
9. For a standard air fryer, mix the chicken with the oil and all the spices.
10. Preheat the air fryer oven to 260°C. Put the chicken breasts in the tray with all the vegetables and pour the chicken broth and soup over it. Air fry for 20 minutes, add in the cream and air fry for a further 5 minutes.
11. Enjoy!

Nutrition:
Calories: 568
Total Fat: 31.1 g
Saturated Fat: 9.1 g
Cholesterol: 95 mg
Sodium: 1111 mg
Total Carbohydrate: 50.8 g
Dietary Fiber: 3.9 g
Total Sugars: 18.8 g
Protein: 23.4 g

153. Chicken Casserole

Preparation Time: 10 Minutes
Cooking Time: 9 minutes
Servings: 6

Ingredients:

- 3 cups cooked chicken, shredded
- 12 oz. bag egg noodles
- ½ large onion
- ½ cup chopped carrots
- ¼ cup frozen peas
- ¼ cup frozen broccoli pieces
- 2 stalks celery chopped
- 5 cups chicken broth
- 1 tsp. garlic powder
- Salt and pepper, to taste
- 1 cup cheddar cheese, shredded
- 1 package French's onions
- ¼ cup sour cream
- 1 can cream of chicken and mushroom soup

Directions:

1. Add the chicken, chicken broth, black pepper, salt, garlic powder, vegetables, and egg noodles to the Instant Pot Duo.
2. Please put on the pressure-cooking lid and seal it.
3. Hit the "Pressure Button" and select 4 minutes of cooking time, then press "Start."
4. Once the Instant Pot Duo beeps, do a quick release and remove its lid.
5. Stir in cheese, 1/3 of French's onions, the can of soup and sour cream.
6. Mix well and spread the remaining onion on top.
7. Put on the Air Fryer lid and seal it.
8. Press the "Air fryer Button" and select 5 minutes of cooking time, then press "Start."
9. Once the Instant Pot Duo beeps, remove its lid.
10. Serve.
11. For a standard air fryer, mix the chicken, chicken broth, black pepper, salt, garlic powder, vegetables, and egg noodles in the air fryer pan. Preheat the air fryer oven to 260°C.
12. Place the chicken mixture in the air fryer and air fry for 15 minutes.
13. Stir in cheese, 1/3 of French's onions, the can of soup and sour cream.
14. Mix well and spread the remaining onion on top. Air fry for a further 5 minutes.
15. Serve.

Nutrition:

Calories: 494
Total Fat: 19.1 g
Saturated Fat: 9.6 g
Cholesterol: 142 mg
Sodium: 1233 mg
Total Carbohydrate: 29 g
Dietary Fiber: 2.6 g
Total Sugars: 3.7 g
Protein: 48.9 g

154. Ranch Chicken Wings

Preparation Time: 10 minutes
Cooking Time: 35 minutes
Servings: 6

Ingredients:

- 12 chicken wings
- 1 Tbsp. olive oil
- 1 cup chicken broth
- ¼ cup butter
- ½ cup Red Hot Sauce
- ¼ tsp. Worcestershire sauce
- 1 Tbsp. white vinegar
- ¼ tsp. cayenne pepper
- 1/8 tsp. garlic powder
- Seasoned salt, to taste
- Ranch dressing for dipping.
- Celery, for garnish

Directions:

1. Set the Air Fryer Basket in the Instant Pot Duo and pour the broth into it.
2. Spread the chicken wings in the basket and put on the pressure-cooking lid.
3. Hit the "Pressure Button" and select 10 minutes of cooking time, then press "Start."
4. Meanwhile, for the sauce, add butter, vinegar, cayenne pepper, garlic powder, Worcestershire sauce, and spicy sauce in a small saucepan.
5. Stir and cook this sauce for 5 minutes on medium heat until it thickens.
6. Once the Instant Pot Duo beeps, do a quick release and remove its lid.
7. Remove the wings and empty the Instant Pot Duo.
8. Toss the wings with oil, salt, and black pepper.
9. Set the Air Fryer Basket in the Instant Pot Duo and arrange the wings into it.
10. Put on the Air Fryer lid and seal it.
11. Press the "Air Fryer Button" and select 20 minutes of cooking time, then press "Start."
12. Once the Instant Pot Duo beeps, remove its lid.
13. Transfer the wings to the sauce and mix well.
14. Serve.
15. For a standard air fryer, place the chicken wings in an air fryer pan and mix it with the broth.
16. Preheat the air fryer oven to 260°C.
17. Place the pan with the wings in the air fryer and cook for 7 minutes.

18. Remove the wings from the pan and discard the broth. Toss the wings with oil, salt and black pepper.
19. Place the wings in the air fryer basket and bake for a further 8 minutes.
20. Meanwhile, for the sauce, add butter, vinegar, cayenne pepper, garlic powder, Worcestershire sauce, and spicy sauce in a small saucepan.
21. Stir and cook this sauce for 5 minutes on medium heat until it thickens.
22. Once the wings are cooked, transfer the wings to the sauce and mix well.
23. Serve.

Nutrition:
Calories: 414
Total Fat: 31.6 g
Saturated Fat: 11 g
Cholesterol: 98 mg
Sodium: 568 mg
Total Carbohydrate: 11.2 g
Dietary Fiber: 0.3 g
Total Sugars: 0.2 g
Protein: 20.4 g

155.Chicken Mac and Cheese

Preparation Time: 10 minutes
Cooking Time: 9 minutes
Servings: 6

Ingredients:
- 2 ½ cup whole-wheat macaroni
- 2 cup chicken stock
- 1 cup cooked chicken, shredded
- 1 ¼ cup heavy cream
- 8 Tbsps. butter
- 2 2/3 cups cheddar cheese, shredded
- 1/3 cup Parmesan cheese, shredded
- 1 bag whole-wheat Ritz crackers
- ¼ tsp garlic powder
- Salt and pepper, to taste

Directions:
1. Add chicken stock, heavy cream, chicken, 4 Tbsp. butter, and macaroni to the Instant Pot Duo.
2. Put on the pressure-cooking lid and seal it.
3. Hit the "Pressure Button" and select 4 minutes of cooking time, then press "Start."
4. Crush the crackers and mix them well with 4 Tbsp. of melted butter.
5. Once the Instant Pot Duo beeps, do a quick release and remove its lid.
6. Layer the crackers and all the cheese over the chicken mixture. Put on the Air Fryer lid and seal it.
7. Press the "Air Fryer Button" and select 5 minutes of cooking time, then press "Start."
8. Once the Instant Pot Duo beeps, remove its lid.
9. Serve.
24. For a standard air fryer, preheat the air fryer oven to 260°C.
10. Add chicken stock, heavy cream, chicken, 4 Tbsp. butter, and macaroni to an air fryer pan and cook for 8 minutes.
11. Crush the crackers and mix them well with 4 Tbsp. of melted butter.
12. After 8 minutes layer the crackers and all the cheese over the chicken mixture and cook for a further 5 minutes.
13. Serve.

Nutrition:
Calories: 611
Total Fat: 43.6 g
Saturated Fat: 26.8 g
Cholesterol: 147 mg
Sodium: 739 mg
Total Carbohydrate: 29.5 g
Dietary Fiber: 1.2 g
Total Sugars: 1.7 g
Protein: 25.4 g

156.Instant Pot Broccoli Chicken Casserole

Preparation Time: 10 minutes
Cooking Time: 22 minutes
Servings: 6

Ingredients:
- 1 ½ lb. chicken, cubed
- 2 tsp. chopped garlic
- 2 Tbsp. butter
- 1 ½ cups chicken broth
- 1 ½ cups long-grain brown rice
- 1 (10.75 oz.) can cream of chicken soup
- 2 cups broccoli florets
- 1 cup crushed whole-wheat Ritz cracker
- 2 Tbsp. melted butter
- 2 cups shredded cheddar cheese

Directions:
1. Place 1 cup water in the Instant Pot Duo and place a basket in it.
2. Place the broccoli in the basket evenly.
3. Put on the pressure-cooking lid and seal it.
4. Hit the “Pressure Button” and select 1 minute of cooking time, then press “Start.” Once the Instant Pot Duo beeps, do a quick release and remove its lid.
5. Remove the broccoli and empty the Instant Pot Duo. Hit the sauté button, then add 2 Tbsps. of butter.

6. Toss in chicken, stir to cook for 5 minutes, and add garlic and sauté for 30 seconds.
7. Stir in rice, chicken broth, and cream of chicken soup.
8. Put on the pressure-cooking lid and seal it. Hit the "Pressure Button" and select 12 minutes of cooking time, then press "Start."
9. Once the Instant Pot Duo beeps, do a quick release and remove its lid.
10. Add cheese and broccoli, then mix well gently.
11. Toss the cracker with 2 Tbsps. of butter in a bowl and spread over the chicken.
12. Close the Air Fryer lid. Press the "Air Fryer Button" and select 4 minutes of cooking time, then press "Start."
13. Once the Instant Pot Duo beeps, remove its lid.
14. Serve.

Nutrition:
Calories: 609
Total Fat: 24.4 g
Saturated Fat: 12.6 g
Cholesterol: 142 mg
Sodium: 924 mg
Total Carbohydrate: 45.5 g
Dietary Fiber: 1.4 g
Total Sugars: 1.6 g
Protein: 49.2 g

157. Chicken Tikka Kebab

Preparation Time: 10 minutes
Cooking Time: 17 minutes
Servings: 4

Ingredients:

- 1 lb. chicken thighs, boneless skinless, cubed
- 1 Tbsp. oil
- ½ cup red onion, cubed
- ½ cup green bell pepper, cubed
- ½ cup red bell pepper, cubed
- Lime wedges to garnish
- Onion rounds to garnish

For marinade:

- ½ cup Greek yogurt
- ¾ Tbsp. ginger, grated
- ¾ Tbsp. garlic, minced
- 1 Tbsp. lime juice
- 2 tsp. red chili powder mild
- ½ tsp. ground turmeric
- 1 tsp. garam masala
- 1 tsp. coriander powder
- ½ Tbsp. dried fenugreek leaves
- 1 tsp. salt

Directions:

1. Prepare the marinade by mixing yogurt with all its ingredients in a bowl.
2. Fold in chicken, then mix well to coat and refrigerate for 8 hours.
3. Add bell pepper, onions, and oil to the marinade, and mix well.
4. Thread the chicken, peppers, and onions alternatively on the skewers.
5. Place the Air Fryer Basket in the air fryer and preheat the air fryer oven to 260°C.
6. Place the skewers in the air fryer basket and select 8 minutes of cooking time, then press "Start."
7. Flip the skewers after 8 minutes and continue Air frying for 7 minutes.
8. Serve.

Nutrition:
Calories: 241
Total Fat: 14.2 g
Saturated Fat: 3.8 g
Cholesterol: 92 mg
Sodium: 695 mg
Total Carbohydrate: 8.5 g
Dietary Fiber: 1.6 g
Total Sugars: 3.9 g
Protein: 21.8 g

158. Bacon-Wrapped Chicken

Preparation Time: 10 minutes
Cooking Time: 24 minutes
Servings: 4

Ingredients:

- ¼ cup maple syrup
- 1 tsp. ground black pepper
- 1 tsp. Dijon mustard
- ¼ tsp. garlic powder
- 1/8 tsp. kosher salt
- 4 (6 oz.) skinless, boneless chicken breasts
- 8 slices bacon

Directions:

1. Preheat the air fryer oven to 260°C.
2. Whisk maple syrup with salt, garlic powder, mustard, and black pepper in a small bowl.
3. Rub the chicken with salt and black pepper and wrap each chicken breast with two slices of bacon.
4. Place the wrapped chicken in the air fryer baking pan.
5. Brush the wrapped chicken with maple syrup mixture.
6. Select 20 minutes of cooking times, then press "Start."
7. Once the function is completed, switch the air fryer to Broil mode and broil for 4 minutes.
8. Serve.

Nutrition:
Calories: 441
Total Fat: 18.3 g
Saturated Fat: 5.2 g
Cholesterol: 141 mg
Sodium: 1081 mg
Total Carbohydrate: 14 g
Dietary Fiber: 0.1 g
Total Sugars: 11.8 g
Protein: 53.6 g

159. Creamy Chicken Thighs

Preparation Time: 10 minutes
Cooking Time: 25 minutes
Servings: 6

Ingredients:

- 1 Tbsp. olive oil
- 6 chicken thighs, bone-in, skin-on
- Salt
- Freshly ground black pepper
- 2 cloves garlic, minced
- 1 Tbsp. fresh thyme leaves
- 1 tsp. crushed red pepper flakes
- 3/4 cup low-sodium chicken broth
- 1/2 cup heavy cream
- 1/2 cup sun-dried tomatoes, chopped
- 1/4 cup Parmesan, grated
- Freshly torn basil, for serving

Directions:

1. Preheat the air fryer oven to 260°C.
2. Rub chicken with oil, salt, and black, place in the air fryer pan and sear for 5 minutes per side.
3. Add broth, cream, Parmesan, spices, and tomatoes.
4. S Select 20 minutes of cooking time, then press "Start."
5. Once done, garnish with basil and serve.

Nutrition:
Calories: 454
Total Fat: 37.8 g
Saturated Fat: 14.4 g
Cholesterol: 169 mg
Sodium: 181 mg
Total Carbohydrate: 2.8 g
Dietary Fiber: 0.7 g
Total Sugars: 0.7 g
Protein: 26.9 g

160. Lemon Pepper Chicken

Preparation Time: 1 hour and 10 minutes
Cooking Time: 28 minutes
Servings: 4

Ingredients:

- 4 pastured chicken breasts
- ¼ cup lemon juice
- 3 Tbsps. lemon-pepper seasoning
- 2 tips. Worcestershire sauce
- ¼ cup olive oil

Directions:

1. Prepare the marinade: place oil, Worcestershire sauce, salt, and lemon juice in a bowl, and whisk until combined.
2. Cut each chicken breast into four pieces, add the chicken pieces into the marinade, toss until well coated, and marinate the chicken in the refrigerator for a minimum of 1 hour. Then, switch on the air fryer, insert the fryer basket, grease it with olive oil, then shut the lid, set the fryer at 350°F, and preheat for 5 minutes.
3. Open the fryer, add half the chicken pieces in a single layer, spray with oil, close the lid, and cook for 14 minutes at 350°F until nicely golden and cooked, turning the chicken halfway through the frying.
4. When the air fryer beeps, open its lid, transfer chicken onto a serving plate, and cook the remaining chicken pieces in the same manner. Serve hot.

Nutrition:
Calories: 55
Carbs: 1.3 g
Fat: 2.7 g
Protein: 6.6 g

161. Crumbed Poultry Tenderloins

Preparation Time: 15 minutes
Cooking Time: 12 minutes
Servings: 1

Ingredients:

- 1 egg
- ½ cup dry bread crumbs
- 2 Tbsp. Vegetable oil
- 8 chicken tenderloins

Directions:

1. Set the air fryer temperature to 350°F.
2. Wisk the egg in a small dish. Mix bread crumbs and oil in a second bowl until the mixture becomes loosened and crumbly.
3. Dip each poultry tenderloin into the egg dish and right into the crumb mix, making sure it is

uniformly covered. Lay poultry tenderloins into the basket of the air fryer.

4. Cook till no longer pink in the center, about 12 mins. An instant-read thermometer inserted right into the center needs to read at least 165°F.

Nutrition:
Calories: 253
Carbs: 9.8 g
Protein: 26.2
Fat: 11.4 g

162. Air Fryer Barbeque Cheddar-Stuffed Chicken Breasts

Preparation Time: 10 minutes
Cooking Time: 25 minutes
Servings: 2

Ingredients:

- 5 strips bacon
- 2 oz. cubed cheddar cheese
- ¼ cup sugar-free BBQ sauce, divided
- 4 (4 oz.) skinless, boneless chicken breasts.
- Salt and black pepper

Directions:

1. Adjust the temperature of the air fryer to 380°F. Cook 1 strip of bacon in the air fryer for 2 mins. Remove from the air fryer and cut into small pieces. Line the air fryer and increase the temperature to 400°F.
2. Combine the cooked bacon, cheddar cheese, and 1 Tbsp. BBQ sauce in a bowl.
3. Use a sharp knife to make a horizontal 1-inch cut on top of each breast, producing a little interior pocket. Stuff each breast with the bacon-cheese combination. Wrap a strips of bacon around each chicken breast. Coat the breast with remaining barbecue sauce and place it in the air fryer basket.
4. Cook for 10 minutes in the air fryer, turn and continue cooking until chicken is no longer pink in the center, and the juices run clear, about 10 more minutes. An instant-read thermostat placed into the center needs to read at least 165°F.

Nutrition:
Calories: 379
Carbs: 12.3 g
Protein: 37.7 g
Fat: 18.9 g

163. Air Fryer Chicken Wings

Preparation Time: 5minutes
Cooking Time: 15 minutes
Servings: 4

Ingredients:

- 6 chicken wings, flats and drumettes
- olive oil spray
- Salt
- Pepper
- Barbecue sauce

Directions:

1. Spray the air fryer basket or foil-lined air fryer basket with non-stick cooking spray.
2. Arrange the wings evenly into the basket. In a 4-quart air fryer basket, 6 wings fit well. Re-adjust this as required for the dimension of your air fryer.
3. Spray the wings with olive oil spray, and a sprinkling of salt and pepper to the wings.
4. Cook at 390°F for 10 minutes.
5. Turn and also cook for an extra 10 minutes at 390°F.
6. Make sure the wings' internal temperature goes to the very least 165°F.
7. Coat with BBQ sauce, if you prefer, or other dipping sauces.

Nutrition:
Calories: 308
Protein: 17 g
Fat: 11 g
Carbs: 0 g

164. Buttermilk Brined Turkey Breast

Preparation Time: 15 minutes
Cooking Time: 20 minutes
Servings: 8

Ingredients:

- ¾ cup brine from a can of olives
- 3½ lbs. boneless, skinless turkey breast
- 2 fresh thyme sprigs
- 1 fresh rosemary sprig
- ½ cup buttermilk

Directions:

1. Preheat the Air fryer to 350°F and grease the Air fryer basket.
2. Mix olive brine and buttermilk in a bowl until well combined.
3. Place the turkey breast, buttermilk mixture and herb sprigs in a resealable plastic bag.
4. Seal the bag and refrigerate for about 12 hours.
5. Remove the turkey breast from bag and place the turkey breast in the Air fryer basket.
6. Cook for 15 minutes, flipping once and cook for a further 15 minutes.

7. Transfer the turkey breast onto a cutting board and cut into desired size slices to serve.

Nutrition:
Calories: 215
Fat: 3.5g
Carbohydrates: 9.4g
Sugar: 7.7g
Protein: 34.4g
Sodium: 2000mg

165. Delightful Turkey Wings

Preparation Time: 10 minutes
Cooking Time: 26 minutes
Servings: 4

Ingredients:

- 2 lbs. turkey wings
- 4 Tbsps. chicken seasoning rub
- 3 Tbsps. olive oil

Directions:

1. Preheat the Air fryer to 380°F and grease the Air fryer basket.
2. Mix the turkey wings, chicken rub, and olive oil in a bowl until well combined.
3. Arrange the turkey wings into the Air fryer basket and cook for about 26 minutes, flipping once in between.
4. Place the turkey wings on a platter and serve hot.

Nutrition:
Calories: 204
Fat: 15.5g
Carbohydrates: 3g
Sugar: 0g
Protein: 12g
Sodium: 465mg

166. Duck Rolls

Preparation Time: 20 minutes
Cooking Time: 40 minutes
Servings: 3

Ingredients:

- 2 (1 lb. total) duck breast fillets, each cut into 2 pieces
- 3 Tbsps. fresh parsley, finely chopped
- 1 small red onion, finely chopped
- 1 garlic clove, crushed
- 1½ tsps. ground cumin
- 1 tsp. ground cinnamon
- ½ tsp. red chili powder
- Salt, to taste
- 2 Tbsps. olive oil

Directions:

1. Preheat the Air fryer to 355°F and grease th Air fryer basket.
2. Mix the garlic, parsley, onion, spices, and 1 tablespoon of olive oil in a bowl.
3. Make a slit in each duck piece horizontally and coat with onion mixture.
4. Roll each duck piece tightly and transfer into the Air fryer basket.
5. Cook for about 40 minutes and cut into desired size slices to serve.

Nutrition:
Calories: 239
Fats: 8.2g
Carbohydrates: 3.2g
Sugar: 0.9g
Proteins: 37.5g
Sodium: 46mg

167. Buttered Duck Breasts

Preparation Time: 15 minutes
Cooking Time: 22 minutes
Servings: 4

Ingredients:

- 2 (12 oz.) duck breasts
- 3 Tbsps. unsalted butter, melted
- Salt and ground black pepper, as required
- ½ tsp. dried thyme, crushed
- ¼ tsp. star anise powder

Directions:

1. Preheat the Air fryer to 390°F and grease the air fryer basket.
2. Season the duck breasts generously with salt and black pepper.
3. Arrange the duck breasts in the prepared air fryer basket and cook for about 10 minutes.
4. Dish out the duck breasts and drizzle with melted butter.
5. Season with thyme and star anise powder and place the duck breasts again into the Air fryer basket.
6. Cook for about 12 more minutes and serve warm.

Nutrition:
Calories: 296
Fat: 15.5g
Carbohydrates: 0.1g
Sugar: 0g
Protein: 37.5g
Sodium: 100mg

168. Beer-Coated Duck Breast

Preparation Time: 15 minutes
Cooking Time: 20 minutes
Servings: 2

Ingredients:

- 1 Tbsp. fresh thyme, chopped
- 1 cup beer
- 1 (10 ½ oz.) duck breast

- 6 cherry tomatoes
- 1 Tbsp. olive oil
- 1 tsp. mustard
- Salt and ground black pepper, as required
- 1 Tbsp. balsamic vinegar

Directions:

1. Preheat the Air fryer to 390°F and grease an air fryer basket.
2. Mix the olive oil, mustard, thyme, beer, salt, and black pepper in a bowl.
3. Coat the duck breasts generously with marinade and refrigerate, covered, for about 4 hours.
4. Cover the duck breasts with foil and arrange into the air fryer basket.
5. Cook for about 15 minutes and remove the foil from breast.
6. Set the Air fryer to 355°F and place the duck breast and tomatoes into the air fryer basket.
7. Cook for about 5 minutes and dish out the duck breasts and cherry tomatoes.
8. Drizzle with vinegar and serve immediately.

Nutrition:

Calories: 332
Fat: 13.7g
Carbohydrates: 9.2g
Sugar: 2.5g
Protein: 34.6g
Sodium: 88mg

169. Tender Chicken Teriyaki

Preparation time: 15 minutes
Cooking time: 17 minutes
Servings: 7

Ingredients:

- 3 lbs. chicken breast, skinless, boneless
- ½ cup Teriyaki sauce, sugar-free
- 1 Tbsp. olive oil

Directions:

1. Chop the chicken breast into the cubes and combine together with Teriyaki sauce and olive oil.
2. Mix the chicken mixture well and leave for 10 minutes in the fridge.
3. Then transfer the chicken in the air fryer and flatten gently with a spatula.
4. Cook the meal for 17 minutes at 360°F.

Nutrition:

Calories 257
Fat 6.9 g
Fiber 0 g
Carbs 3.2 g
Protein 42.4 g

170. Garlic Chicken Sandwich

Preparation time: 15 minutes
Cooking time: 10 minutes
Servings: 2

Ingredients:

- 4 lettuce leaves
- 6 oz. chicken fillet
- 1 Tbsp. mayonnaise, sugar-free
- ½ tsp. minced garlic
- ½ tsp. ground nutmeg
- 1 tsp. tomato paste
- 1 tsp. sunflower oil
- 1 tomato, sliced

Directions:

1. In a mixing bowl combine together the sunflower oil, tomato paste, ground nutmeg, and minced garlic.
2. Cut the chicken fillet into 2 servings and rub with the tomato paste mixture.
3. Then place the chicken fillets in the air fryer and cook them for 5 minutes on each side at 390°F.
4. Place the cooked chicken fillets on the 2 lettuce leaves.
5. Top the chicken with sliced tomato, and mayonnaise.
6. Cover the sandwich with remaining lettuce leaves.

Nutrition:

Calories 337
Fat 20.7 g
Fiber 0.7 g
Carbs 4.6 g
Protein 32.2 g

171. Cilantro Chicken Thighs

Preparation time: 10 minutes
Cooking time: 20 minutes
Servings: 2

Ingredients:

- 2 chicken thighs
- 2 oz. celery root, grated
- 1 Tbsp. lemon juice
- 1 tsp. chili powder
- ½ tsp. dried oregano
- ½ tsp. dried cilantro
- 1 Tbsp. avocado oil
- ½ tsp. salt

Directions:

1. Mix together grated celery root, lemon juice, chili powder, dried oregano, cilantro, salt, and avocado oil.
2. Carefully rub the chicken thighs with celery root mixture. Let sit for 20 minutes to marinate.
3. Transfer the chicken thighs to the air fryer and cook for 20 minutes at 365°F.

Nutrition:

Calories 306
Fat 12.1 g

Fiber 1.5 g
Carbs 4.1 g
Protein 43 g

172. Coriander Chicken

Preparation time: 10 minutes
Cooking time: 15 minutes
Servings: 4
Ingredients:

- 8 oz. chicken fillet, chopped
- 1 tsp. ground coriander
- 1 Tbsp. fresh cilantro, chopped
- 1 tsp. salt
- 1 tsp. ground turmeric
- 1 tsp. minced garlic
- ½ tsp. minced ginger
- 5 Tbsps. oatmeal
- ¼ cup water
- 1 onion, sliced
- Cooking spray

Directions:

1. Grind together ground coriander, cilantro, and salt.
2. Place the chicken in the bowl and sprinkle with grinded spices.
3. Add the ground turmeric, minced garlic, ginger, onion, and oatmeal. Stir the mixture well. Add water and stir the mixture until smooth. Add more water if desired.
4. Place the chopped chicken mixture in the air fryer.
5. Cook for 15 minutes at 375°F. Stir the chicken every 5 minutes.

Nutrition:
Calories 147
Fat 4.7 g
Fiber 1.4 g
Carbs 7.7 g
Protein 17.6 g

173. Chicken Tenders

Preparation time: 10 minutes
Cooking time: 12 minutes
Servings: 2
Ingredients:

- 11 oz. chicken fillet
- 5 pecans
- ¼ cup almond flour
- 1 egg, beaten
- ½ tsp. salt
- 1 tsp. sunflower oil

Directions:

1. Cut the chicken into tenders and sprinkle with salt.
2. Dip the chicken tenders in egg and cover well.
3. Grind pecans and combine them with almond flour.
4. Coat every chicken tender in the pecan mixture.
5. Transfer the chicken tenders in the air fryer and sprinkle with sunflower oil.
6. Cook the meal for 12 minutes, 6 minutes on each side at 390°F.

Nutrition:
Calories 368
Fat 23.9 g
Fiber 2.2 g
Carbs 8 g
Protein 31.3 g

174. Sage Chicken Breast

Preparation time: 10 minutes
Cooking time: 40 minutes
Servings: 6
Ingredients:

- 18 oz. chicken breast, boneless
- 2 Tbsps. sage
- 1 Tbsp. olive oil

Directions:

1. Make several small cuts in the chicken breast and drizzle with olive oil. Rub the chicken with sage and transfer to the air fryer.
2. Cook for 30 minutes at 385°F.
3. Then flip the chicken over and cook for 10 minutes more.

Nutrition:
Calories 119
Fat 4.5 g
Fiber 0.3 g
Carbs 0.4 g
Protein 18.1 g

175. Duck Breast with Figs

Preparation Time: 20 minutes
Cooking Time: 45 minutes
Servings: 2
Ingredients:

- 1 lb. boneless duck breast
- 6 fresh figs, halved
- 1 Tbsp. fresh thyme, chopped
- 2 cups fresh pomegranate juice
- 2 Tbsps. lemon juice
- 2 Tbsps. brown sugar substitute
- 1 tsp. olive oil
- Salt and black pepper, as required

Directions:

1. Preheat the air fryer to 400°F and grease the air fryer basket.
2. Put the pomegranate juice, lemon juice, and brown sugar in a medium saucepan over medium heat. Bring to a boil and simmer on low heat for about 25 minutes.

3. Season the duck breasts generously with salt and black pepper.
4. Arrange the duck breasts into the air fryer basket, skin side up and cook for about 14 minutes, flipping once in between.
5. Let the duck breasts rest on a cutting board for about 10 minutes.
6. Meanwhile, put the figs, olive oil, salt, and black pepper in a bowl and mix well.
7. Set the air fryer to 400ºF and arrange the figs into the Air fryer basket. Cook for about 5 more minutes and transfer to a platter.
8. Put the duck breast ovr the roasted figs and drizzle with warm pomegranate juice mixture.
9. Garnish with fresh thyme and serve warm.

Nutrition:

Calories: 699
Fat: 12.1g
Carbohydrates: 90g
Sugar: 74g
Protein: 519g
Sodium: 110mg

176. Herbed Duck Legs

Preparation Time: 10 minutes
Cooking Time: 30 minutes
Servings: 2

Ingredients:

- ½ Tbsp. fresh thyme, chopped
- ½ Tbsp. fresh parsley, chopped
- 2 duck legs
- 1 garlic clove, minced
- 1 tsp. five spice powder
- Salt and black pepper, as required

Directions:

1. Preheat the Air fryer to 340ºF and grease the air fryer basket.
2. Mix the garlic, herbs, five spice powder, salt, and black pepper in a bowl.
3. Rub the duck legs with garlic mixture generously and arrange in the air fryer basket.
4. Cook for about 25 minutes and set the air fryer to 390ºF.
5. Cook for 5 more minutes, then serve hot.

Nutrition:

Calories: 138
Fat: 4.5g
Carbohydrates: 1g
Sugar: 0g
Protein: 25g
Sodium: 82mg

177. Chicken Wings with Prawn Paste

Preparation Time: 20 minutes
Cooking Time: 8 minutes
Servings: 6

Ingredients:

- Corn flour, as required
- 2 lbs. chicken wings
- 2 Tbsps. prawn paste
- 4 Tbsps. olive oil
- 1½ tsps. sugar
- 2 tsps. sesame oil
- 1 tsp. Shaoxing wine
- 2 tsps. fresh ginger juice

Directions:

1. Mix all the ingredients in a bowl except wings and corn flour.
2. Rub the chicken wings generously with marinade and refrigerate overnight.
3. Coat the chicken wings evenly with corn flour and set aside.
4. Set the air fryer to 390ºF and arrange the chicken wings in the air fryer basket.
5. Cook for about 8 minutes and serve hot.

Nutrition:

Calories: 416
Fat: 31.5g
Carbohydrates: 11.2g
Sugar: 1.6g
Protein: 24.4g
Sodium: 661mg

178. Spicy Green Crusted Chicken

Preparation Time: 10 minutes
Cooking Time: 40 minutes
Servings: 6

Ingredients:

- 6 eggs, beaten
- 6 tsps. parsley
- 4 tsps. thyme
- 1 lb. chicken pieces
- 6 tsps. oregano
- Salt and freshly ground black pepper, to taste
- 4 tsps. paprika

Directions:

1. Preheat the air fryer to 360ºF and grease the air fryer basket.
2. Whisk eggs in a bowl and mix all the ingredients in another bowl except chicken pieces.
3. Dip the chicken in the eggs and then coat generously with the dry mixture.
4. Arrange half of the chicken pieces in the air fryer basket and cook for about 20 minutes.
5. Repeat with the remaining chicken and serve hot.

Nutrition:
Calories: 218
Fat: 10.4g
Carbohydrates: 2.6g
Sugar: 0.6g
Protein: 27.9g
Sodium: 128mg

179. Creamy Chicken Tenders

Preparation Time: 15 minutes
Cooking Time: 20 minutes
Servings: 8
Ingredients:

- 2 lbs. chicken tenders
- 1 cup feta cheese
- 4 Tbsps. olive oil
- 1 cup cream
- Salt and black pepper, to taste

Directions:

1. Preheat the air fryer to 340°F and grease the air fryer basket.
2. Season the chicken tenders with salt and black pepper.
3. Arrange the chicken tenders in the air fryer basket and drizzle with olive oil. Cook for about 15 minutes, then set the air fryer at 355°F.
4. Cook for about 5 more minutes.
5. Mix the cream and feta cheese to form a sauce. Place the warm chicken tenders in the sauce and mix well
6. Cook for about 5 more minutes and serve hot.

Nutrition:
Calories: 344
Fat: 21.1g
Carbohydrates: 1.7g
Sugar: 1.4g
Protein: 35.7g
Sodium: 317mg

180. Chicken Breasts with Chimichurri

Preparation Time: 15 minutes
Cooking Time: 35 minutes
Servings: 1
Ingredients:

- 1 chicken breast, bone-in, skin-on

Chimichurri:

- ½ bunch fresh cilantro
- 1/4 bunch fresh parsley
- ½ shallot, peeled, cut in quarters
- ½ Tbsp. paprika ground
- ½ Tbsp. chili powder
- ½ Tbsp. fennel ground
- ½ tsp. black pepper, ground
- ½ tsp. onion powder
- 1 tsp. salt
- ½ tsp. garlic powder
- ½ tsp. cumin ground
- ½ Tbsp. canola oil

Directions:

1. Preheat the air fryer to 300°F and grease the air fryer basket.
2. Combine all the spices in a suitable bowl and season the chicken with it.
3. Drizzle with canola oil and arrange the chicken in the air fryer basket.
4. Cook for about 35 minutes and transfer to a platter.
5. Put all the chimichurri ingredients in a blender and blend until smooth.
6. Serve the chicken with chimichurri sauce.

Nutrition:
Calories: 140
Fats: 7.9g
Carbohydrates: 1.8g
Sugar: 7.1g
Proteins: 7.2g
Sodium: 581mg

181. Fried Chicken Thighs

Preparation Time: 10 minutes
Cooking Time: 25 minutes
Servings: 4
Ingredients:

- ½ cup almond flour
- 1 egg beaten
- 4 small chicken thighs
- 1½ Tbsps. Old Bay Cajun Seasoning
- 1 tsp. seasoning salt

Directions:

1. Preheat the air fryer to 400°F for 3 minutes and grease the air fryer basket.
2. Whisk the egg in a shallow bowl and place the Old Bay, flour and salt in another bowl.
3. Dip the chicken in the egg and coat with the flour mixture.
4. Arrange the chicken thighs in the Air fryer basket and cook for about 25 minutes.
5. Transfer to a platter and serve warm.

Nutrition:
Calories: 180
Fat: 20g
Carbohydrates: 3g
Sugar: 1.2g
Protein: 21g
odium: 686mg

182. Sweet Sriracha Turkey Legs

Preparation Time: 10 minutes
Cooking Time: 35 minutes
Servings: 2
Ingredients:

- 1 lb. turkey legs
- 1 Tbsp. butter
- 1 Tbsp. cilantro
- 1 Tbsp. chives
- 1 Tbsp. scallions
- 4 Tbsps. sriracha sauce
- 1½ Tbsps. soy sauce
- ½ lime, juiced

Directions:

1. Preheat the air fryer on roasting mode to 360°F for 3 minutes and grease the air fryer basket.
2. Arrange the turkey legs in the air fryer basket and cook for about 30 minutes, flipping several times during cooking.
3. Mix butter, scallions, sriracha sauce, soy sauce and lime juice in the saucepan and cook for about for 3 minutes until the sauce thickens.
4. Drizzle this sauce over the turkey legs and garnish with cilantro and chives to serve.

Nutrition:
Calories: 361
Fat: 16.3g
Carbohydrates: 9.3g
Sugar: 18.2g
Protein: 33.3g
Sodium: 515mg

183. Gyro Seasoned Chicken

Preparation Time: 10 minutes
Cooking Time: 30 minutes
Servings: 4
Ingredients:

- 2 lbs. chicken thighs
- 1 Tbsp. avocado oil
- 2 Tbsps. Primal Palate Super Gyro seasoning
- 2 Tbsps. Primal Palate New Bae seasoning
- 1 Tbsp. Himalayan pink salt

Directions:

1. Preheat the air fryer to 350°F and grease the air fryer basket.
2. Rub the chicken with avocado oil and half of the spices.
3. Arrange the chicken thighs in the air fryer basket and cook for about 25 minutes, flipping once.
4. Sprinkle with the remaining seasoning and cook for 5 more minutes.
5. Serve warm.

Nutrition:
Calories: 545
Fat: 36.4g
Carbohydrates: 0.7g
Sugar: 0g
Protein: 42.5g
Sodium: 272mg

184. Special Salsa Chicken Steak

Preparation Time: 10 minutes
Cooking Time: 30 minutes
Servings: 6
Ingredients:

- 2 lbs. chicken steak
- ½ cup shredded Monterey Jack cheese
- 1 cup tomato sauce
- ½ tsp. garlic powder
- 2 cups salsa
- ½ tsp. hot pepper sauce
- Salt and black pepper, to taste

Directions:

1. Preheat the air fryer to 450°F and grease the air fryer basket.
2. Season the chicken steak with garlic powder, salt and black pepper and marinate for about 8 hours.
3. Mix salsa, tomato sauce and hot pepper sauce in a bowl.
4. Arrange the steak pieces in the air fryer basket and drizzle with the salsa mixture.
5. Cook for about 30 minutes and serve hot.

Nutrition:
Calories: 345
Fat: 14.3g
Carbohydrates: 7.6g
Sugar: 4.3g
Protein: 45.1g
Sodium: 828mg

185. ir Fryer Teriyaki Chicken Drumsticks

Preparation Time: 30 minutes
Cooking Time: 20 minutes
Servings: 3

Ingredients:

- 6 chicken drumsticks
- 1 cup teriyaki sauce
- Sesame seeds and organic onions, for garnish

Directions:

1. Mix drumsticks with teriyaki sauce in a zip lock bag. Allow to marinate in the sauce for half an hour.
2. Preheat air fryer to 360°F.
3. Place drumsticks in one layer in the air fryer basket and cook for 20 minutes. Shake the basket a couple of times during the cooking time.

4. Garnish with sesame seeds as well as sliced organic onions.

Nutrition:
Calories: 163
Carbs: 7 g
Protein: 16 g
Fat: 7 g

Chapter 7. Fish and Seafood Recipes

N. 193 Fried Shrimps

N. 195 Grilled Salmon with Lemon

N. 198 Mustard-Crusted Sole

N. 201 Easy Tuna Wraps

N. 207 Asian Sesame Cod

N. 214 Fish and Vegetable Tacos

186.Air Fryer Tilapia

Preparation Time: 10 minutes
Cooking Time: 10 minutes
Servings: 4
Ingredients:

- Cooking spray
- 1 tsp. grated lemon zest
- 1 Tbsp. lemon juice
- 1 tsp. chopped fresh chives
- 1 tsp. chopped fresh parsley
- 1 ¼ lbs. tilapia fillets
- ¼ tsp. garlic powder
- ¼ tsp. onion powder
- ¼ tsp. salt, divided
- 1/8 tsp. hot paprika
- 1/8 tsp. ground white pepper

Directions:

1. Preheat the air fryer to 400°F for about 5 minutes.
2. Grease the fryer basket with cooking spray.
3. Using paper towels, dry the tilapia fillets and coat them with cooking spray.
4. In a bowl, combine the paprika, lemon zest, garlic powder, 1/8 teaspoon salt, onion powder, salt, and white pepper. Mix the fish with the spices until covered evenly.
5. Place the fish in a single layer in the fryer and cook until the fish flakes easily with a fork. The cooking time is about 7 minutes.
6. Serve by drizzling lemon juice over the fillets and adding the remaining 1/8 teaspoon salt.
7. Garnish with the parsley and chives.

Nutrition:
Calories: 145
Fat: 2.6 g
Protein: 29.9 g
Carbohydrates: 1 g
Fiber: 0 g

187.Salmon Cakes

Preparation Time: 15 minutes
Cooking Time: 12 minutes
Servings: 2
Ingredients:

- Cooking spray
- 7.5 oz. salmon, cooked and flaked
- 1 egg
- ½ cup whole-wheat breadcrumbs
- 2 Tbsp. chopped dill
- 2 Tbsp. canola mayonnaise
- 2 tsp. Dijon mustard
- ¼ tsp. ground pepper
- 2 lemon wedges

Directions:

1. Grease the air fryer's basket with cooking spray. Preheat the air fryer to 400°F for about 5 minutes.
2. In a medium bowl, add the dill, panko, mustard, mayonnaise and pepper, mixing all the ingredients.
3. Gently add the flaked salmon and mix everything together.
4. Form four patties.
5. Place the patties in the basket and cook for about 12 minutes at 400°F or until they become golden brown.
6. Serve with lemon wedges.

Nutrition:
Calories: 512
Fat: 23 g
Protein: 50 g
Carbohydrates: 14 g
Fiber: 3 g

188.Paprika Calamari Rings

Preparation time: 15 minutes
Cooking time: 8 minutes
Servings: 2
Ingredients:

- 7 oz. calamari, trimmed
- ¼ tsp. ground paprika
- ¼ tsp. ground turmeric
- ½ tsp. salt
- ½ cup of almond flour
- 1/3 cup coconut milk
- 1 Tbsp. olive oil

Directions:

1. Slice the calamari into rings. Put them in a bowl and add coconut milk. Stir well.
2. In a separate bowl, mix together ground paprika, ground turmeric, salt, and almond flour.
3. Coat each calamari ring in the flour mixture.
4. Then transfer the "rings" to the air fryer basket and drizzle them with olive oil.
5. Close the lid and cook the seafood for 8 minutes at 360°F. Shake the calamari rings after 4 minutes of cooking.

Nutrition:
Calories 363
Fat 11.2
Fiber 3.2
Carbs 52.9
Protein 13.1

189. Parsley Squids

Preparation time: 10 minutes
Cooking time: 20 minutes
Servings: 4
Ingredients:

- 4 squid tubes, trimmed
- ½ yellow onion, diced
- 1 Tbsp. tomato paste
- 1 tsp. garlic, diced
- ½ cup cooked brown rice
- 1 Tbsp. fresh parsley, chopped
- 1 tomato, chopped
- 1 Tbsp. coconut oil

Directions:

1. In a mixing bowl combine together onion, tomato paste, garlic, rice, parsley, and tomato.
2. Fill the squid tubes with rice mixture and secure the edges with toothpicks.
3. After this, brush each squid tube with coconut oil and transfer in the air fryer.
4. Cook the meal for 20 minutes at 365°F. Flip the "tubes" over after 10 minutes of cooking.

Nutrition:
Calories 187
Fat 5.1
Fiber 1
Carbs 21.4
Protein 14.2

190. Teriyaki Cod Fillets

Preparation time: 35 minutes
Cooking time: 7 minutes
Servings: 4
Ingredients:

- 1 lb. cod fillet
- ¼ cup teriyaki sauce, sugar-free
- 1 Tbsp. soy sauce, sugar-free
- ½ tsp. apple cider vinegar
- ½ tsp. chili flakes
- 1 Tbsp. olive oil
- ½ tsp. ground nutmeg
- ½ tsp. fennel seeds

Directions:

1. Make the marinade: in the bowl combine together teriyaki sauce, soy sauce, apple cider vinegar, chili flakes, olive oil, ground nutmeg, and fennel seeds.
2. Cut the cod fillet into servings and place in the marinade.
3. Leave the fish for 30 minutes to marinate.
4. Remove the fillets from the marinade and transfer in the air fryer basket.
5. Close the lid and cook the fish for 3 minutes at 400°F, and then flip the fish over and cook for 4 minutes more.

Nutrition:
Calories 142
Fat 4.7
Fiber 0.2
Carbs 3.4
Protein 21.6

191. Salmon Balls

Preparation time: 30 minutes
Cooking time: 6 minutes
Servings: 2
Ingredients:

- 7 oz. salmon fillet, ground
- 1 Tbsp. chives, chopped
- ½ tsp. garlic powder
- ¼ tsp. salt
- 1 Tbsp. oatmeal
- 1 egg, beaten
- 1 Tbsp. almond flour
- Cooking spray

Directions:

1. In a mixing bowl combine together almond flour, beaten egg, oatmeal, salt, garlic powder, and chives.
2. Mix until homogenous and add ground salmon fillet.
3. Make balls from the fish mixture with your fingers and put them in the freezer for 10-15 minutes.
4. Then transfer the fish balls in the air fryer, spray them with cooking spray and close the lid.
5. Cook the balls for 6 minutes at 400°F.

Nutrition:
Calories 198
Fat 8.8
Fiber 0.6
Carbs 6.4
Protein 23.5

192. Salmon Cream

Preparation time: 20 minutes
Cooking time: 9 minutes
Servings: 4
Ingredients:

- 11 oz. salmon fillet
- ¼ tsp. ground nutmeg
- ¼ tsp. dried oregano
- 1 tsp. olive oil
- 1 Tbsp. coconut butter
- 1 Tbsp. dill, chopped
- ½ Tbsp. lemon juice
- ½ tsp. chili powder

Directions:

1. Rub the salmon fillet with ground nutmeg, oregano, and brush with olive oil.
2. Arrange the fish fillet in the air fryer and close the lid.
3. Cook the fillet for 7 minutes at 390°F.
4. Then flip the fillet over and cook for 2 minutes more.
5. After this, transfer the cooked fish fillet to a bowl and shred it well with two forks.
6. Add coconut butter, dill, lemon juice, and chili powder. Stir the mixture well to form a pate.
7. Refrigerate the pate for 10-15 minutes before serving.

Nutrition:

Calories 143
Fat 9
Fiber 0.3
Carbs 0.8
Protein 15.4

193.Fried Shrimps

Preparation time: 5 minutes
Cooking time: 4 minutes
Servings: 2
Ingredients:

- 10 oz. shrimp, peeled
- 1 Tbsp. sesame oil
- 1 Tbsp. lemon juice
- ½ tsp. chili powder

Directions:

1. In a mixing bowl combine together shrimps, sesame oil, and chili powder.
2. Shake the shrimp well and transfer in the air fryer in one layer.
3. Close the lid and cook the shrimps for 4 minutes at 400°F. Shake the shrimps after 3 minutes of cooking.
4. Then transfer the cooked seafood to a plate and sprinkle with lemon juice.

Nutrition:

Calories 232
Fat 9.4
Fiber 0.3
Carbs 2.7
Protein 32.4

194.Garlic Trout

Preparation time: 15 minutes
Cooking time: 10 minutes
Servings: 5
Ingredients:

- 1 ½ lbs. trout, trimmed, or use 5 big trout fillets
- 1 oz. lemongrass, chopped
- 4 garlic cloves, peeled, chopped
- 2 Tbsps. olive oil
- 1 tsp. salt

Directions:

1. Rub the trout with salt and fill with garlic and lemongrass.
2. Then brush the fish with olive oil and secure the fish cut with a toothpick.
3. Arrange the fish in the air fryer and cook at 375°F for 10 minutes.

Nutrition:

Calories 316
Fat 17.2
Fiber 0.1
Carbs 2.2
Protein 36.5

195.Grilled Salmon with Lemon

Preparation Time: 9 minutes
Cooking Time: 8 minutes
Servings: 4
Ingredients:

- 2 Tbsp. of olive oil
- 2 salmon fillets
- ⅓ cup of lemon juice
- ⅓ cup of water
- ⅓ cup of gluten-free light soy sauce
- ⅓ cup of honey
- Scallion slices to garnish
- Freshly ground black pepper, garlic powder, and kosher salt to taste

Directions:

1. Season the salmon with salt and pepper.
2. In a bowl, mix soy sauce, water, honey, lemon juice, and oil. Add the salmon to this marinade and let it marinate for at least 2 hours.
3. Let the air fryer preheat at 180°C.
4. Place fish in the air fryer and cook for about 8 minutes.
5. Move to a dish and top with scallion slices.

Nutrition:

Calories: 211
Fat: 9 g
Carbs: 4.9 g
Proteins: 15 g

196.Air-Fried Fish Nuggets

Preparation Time: 15 minutes
Cooking Time: 12 minutes
Servings: 4
Ingredients:

- 2 cups skinless fish fillets, cubed
- 1 beaten egg

- 5 Tbsp. flour
- 5 Tbsp. water
- Kosher salt and pepper, to taste
- ½ cup breadcrumbs mix
- Oil for spraying

Directions:

1. Season the fish cubes with kosher salt and pepper.
2. In a bowl, add the flour and gradually add water, mixing it well.
3. Mix in the egg. Keep mixing but do not over mix.
4. Coat the cubes in batter, then in the breadcrumb mix. Coat well.
5. Place the cubes in a baking tray and spray with oil.
6. Let the air fryer preheat to 200°C.
7. Place cubes in the air fryer and cook for about 12 minutes, or until well cooked and golden brown.
8. Serve with salad greens.

Nutrition:
Calories: 184
Fat: 3 g
Carbs: 10 g
Proteins: 19 g

197.Garlic Rosemary Grilled Prawns

Preparation Time: 5 minutes
Cooking Time: 11 minutes
Servings: 2

Ingredients:

- ½ Tbsp. melted butter
- 8 green capsicum slices
- 8 prawns
- ⅛ cup rosemary leaves
- Kosher salt and freshly ground black pepper
- 3-4 cloves minced garlic

Directions:

1. In a bowl, mix all the ingredients and marinate the prawns in it for at least 60 minutes or more. Add 2 prawns and 2 slices of capsicum on each skewer.
2. Let the air fryer preheat to 180°C.
3. Cook for about 5 to 6 minutes. Then change the temperature to 200°C and cook for another 5 minutes.
4. Serve with lemon wedges.

Nutrition:
Calories: 194
Fat: 10 g
Carbs: 12 g
Proteins: 26 g
Protein: 6g

198.Mustard-Crusted Sole

Preparation Time: 5 Minutes
Cooking Time: 8 to 11 Minutes
Servings: 4

Ingredients:

- 5 tsp. low-sodium yellow mustard
- 1 Tbsp. freshly squeezed lemon juice
- 4 (3 ½ oz./99 g) sole fillets
- ½ tsp. dried thyme
- ½ tsp. dried marjoram
- 1/8 tsp. freshly ground black pepper
- 1 slice low-sodium whole-wheat bread, crumbled
- 2 tsp. olive oil

Directions:

1. In a small bowl, blend the mustard and lemon juice. Spread this evenly over the fillets. Place them in the air fryer basket.
2. In another small bowl, mix the thyme, marjoram, pepper, bread crumbs, and olive oil. Mix until combined.
3. Gently but firmly, press the spice mixture onto each fish fillets top.
4. Bake at 320°F (160°C) for 8 to 11 minutes, or until the fish reaches an inner temperature of at least 145°F (63°C) on a meat thermometer, and the topping is browned and crisp. Serve immediately.

Nutrition:
Calories: 143
Fat: 4 g
Protein: 20 g
Carbs: 5 g
Fiber: 1 g
Sugar 1 g
Sodium: 140 mg

199.Almond Crusted Cod with Chips

Preparation Time: 10 Minutes
Cooking Time: 11 to 15 Minutes
Servings: 4

Ingredients:

- 2 russet potatoes, peeled, thinly sliced, rinsed, and patted dry
- 1 egg white
- 1 Tbsp. freshly squeezed lemon juice
- 1/3 cup ground almonds
- 2 slices low-sodium whole-wheat bread, finely crumbled
- ½ tsp. dried basil
- 4 (4 oz./113 g) cod fillets

Directions:

1. Preheat the oven to 390°F.

2. Put the potato slices in the air fryer basket and air fry at 390°F (199°C) for 11 to 15 minutes, or until crisp and brown. With tongs, turn the fries twice during cooking.
3. In the meantime, in a deep bowl, beat the egg white and lemon juice until frothy.
4. On a plate, mix the almonds, bread crumbs, and basil.
5. One at a time, dip the fillets into the egg white mixture and then into the almond-bread crumb mixture to coat. Place the coated fillets on a wire rack to dry while the fries cook.
6. When the potatoes are done, transfer them to a baking sheet and keep warm in the oven on low heat.
7. Air fry the fish in the air fryer basket for 10 to 14 minutes, or until the fish reaches an internal temperature of at least 140°F (60°C) on a meat thermometer and the coating is browned and crisp. Serve immediately with the potatoes.

Nutrition:
Calories: 248
Fat: 5 g
Protein: 27 g
Carbs: 25 g
Fiber: 3 g
Sugar 3 g
Sodium: 131 mg

200. Honey Lemon Snapper with Fruit

Preparation Time: 15 Minutes
Cooking Time: 9 to 13 Minutes
Servings: 4

Ingredients:

- 4 (4 oz./113 g) red snapper fillets
- 2 tsp. olive oil
- 3 nectarines, halved and pitted
- 3 plums, halved and pitted
- 1 cup red grapes
- 1 Tbsp. freshly squeezed lemon juice
- 1 Tbsp. honey
- ½ tsp. dried thyme

Directions:

1. Put the red snapper in the air fryer basket and drizzle with the olive oil. Air fry at 390°F (199°C) for 4 minutes.
2. Remove the basket and add the nectarines and plums. Scatter the grapes over all.
3. Drizzle with the lemon juice and honey, and sprinkle with the thyme.
4. Transfer again the basket to the air fryer and air fry for 5 to 9 minutes more, or till the fish flakes when tested with a fork, and the fruit is tender. Serve immediately.

Nutrition:
Calories: 246
Fat: 4 g
Protein: 25 g
Carbs: 28 g
Fiber: 3 g
Sugar 24 g
Sodium: 73 mg

201. Easy Tuna Wraps

Preparation Time: 10 Minutes
Cooking Time: 4 to 7 Minutes
Servings: 4

Ingredients:

- 1 lb. (454 g) fresh tuna steak, cut into 1-inch cubes
- 1 Tbsp. grated fresh ginger
- 2 garlic cloves, minced
- ½ tsp. toasted sesame oil
- 4 low-sodium whole-wheat tortillas
- ¼ cup low-fat mayonnaise
- 2 cups shredded romaine lettuce
- 1 red bell pepper, thinly sliced

Directions:

1. In a medium bowl, mix the tuna, ginger, garlic, and sesame oil. Let it stand for 10 minutes, then transfer to the air fryer basket.
2. Air fry at 390°F (199°C) for 4 to 7 minutes, or until done to your liking and lightly browned.
3. Make wraps with tuna, tortillas, mayonnaise, lettuce, and bell pepper. Serve immediately.

Nutrition:
Calories: 289
Fat: 7 g
Protein: 31 g
Carbs: 26 g
Fiber: 1 g
Sugar 1 g
Sodium: 135 mg

202. Asian-Inspired Swordfish Steaks

Preparation Time: 10 Minutes
Cooking Time: 9 to 11 Minutes
Servings: 4

Ingredients:

- 4 (4 oz./113 g) swordfish steaks
- ½ tsp. toasted sesame oil
- 1 jalapeño pepper, finely minced
- 2 garlic cloves, grated
- 1 Tbsp. grated fresh ginger
- ½ tsp. Chinese five-spice powder
- 1/8 tsp. freshly ground black pepper
- 2 Tbsp. freshly squeezed lemon juice

Directions:

1. Place the swordfish steaks on a work surface and drizzle with the sesame oil.
2. In a small bowl, mix the jalapeño, garlic, ginger, five-spice powder, pepper, and lemon juice.
3. Rub this mixture into the fish and let it stand for 10 minutes.
4. Put in the air fryer basket.
5. Roast at 380°F (193°C) for 9 to 11 minutes, or until the swordfish reaches an inner temperature of at least 140°F (60°C) on a meat thermometer. Serve immediately.

Nutrition:
Calories: 188
Fat: 6 g
Protein: 29 g
Carbs: 2 g
Fiber: 0 g
Sugar 1 g
Sodium: 132 mg

203. Salmon with Fennel and Carrot

Preparation Time: 15 Minutes
Cooking Time: 13 to 14 Minutes
Servings: 2

Ingredients:

- 1 fennel bulb, thinly sliced
- 1 large carrot, peeled and sliced
- 1 small onion, thinly sliced
- ¼ cup low-fat sour cream
- ¼ tsp. coarsely ground pepper
- 2 (5 oz./142 g) salmon fillets

Directions:

1. Combine the fennel, carrot, and onion in a bowl, and toss.
2. Put the vegetable mixture into a baking pan. Cook in the air fryer at 400°F (204°C) for 4 minutes, or until the vegetables are crisp-tender.
3. Remove the pan from the air fryer. Stir in the sour cream and sprinkle the vegetables with pepper.
4. Top with the salmon fillets.
5. Return the pan to the air fryer. Roast for another 9 to 10 minutes, or until the salmon just barely flakes when tested with a fork.

Nutrition:
Calories: 254
Fat: 9 g
Protein: 31 g
Carbs: 12 g
Fiber: 3 g
Sugar 5 g
Sodium: 115 mg

204. Ranch Tilapia fillets

Preparation Time: 7 Minutes
Cooking Time: 17 Minutes
Servings: 2 fillets

Ingredients:

- 2 Tbsp. flour
- 1 egg, lightly beaten
- 1 cup crushed cornflakes
- 2 Tbsp. ranch seasoning
- 2 tilapia fillets
- Olive oil spray

Directions:

1. Place a parchment liner in the air fryer basket.
2. Scoop the flour out onto a plate; set it aside.
3. Put the beaten egg in a shallow bowl.
4. Place the cornflakes in a zip-top bag and crush them with a rolling pin or another small, blunt object.
5. On another plate, mix to combine the crushed cereal and ranch seasoning.
6. Dredge the tilapia fillets in the flour, dip in the egg, and press into the cornflake mixture.
7. Place the prepared fillets on the liner in the air fryer in a single layer.
8. Spray lightly with olive oil, and air fry at 400°F (204°C) for 8 minutes. Carefully flip the fillets and spray with more oil. Air fry for an additional 9 minutes, until golden and crispy, then serve.

Nutrition:
Calories: 395
Fat: 7 g
Protein: 34 g
Carbs: 49 g
Fiber: 3 g
Sugar 4 g
Sodium: 980 mg

205. Chilean Sea Bass with Green Olive Relish

Preparation Time: 10 Minutes
Cooking Time: 16 to 20 Minutes
Servings: 4

Ingredients:
Olive oil spray

- 2 (6 oz./170 g) Chilean sea bass fillets, or other firm-fleshed white fish
- 3 Tbsp. extra-virgin olive oil
- ½ tsp. ground cumin
- ½ tsp. kosher salt
- ½ tsp. black pepper
- 1/3 cup pitted green olives, diced
- ¼ cup finely diced onion
- 1 tsp. chopped capers

Directions:

1. Spray the air fryer basket with olive oil spray. Drizzle the fillets with olive oil and sprinkle with cumin, salt, and pepper. Place the fish in the air fryer basket. Bake at 325°F (163°C) for 10 minutes or until the fish flakes easily with a fork.
2. In the meantime, in a small bowl, stir together the olives, onion, and capers.
3. Serve the fish topped with the relish.

Nutrition:
Calories: 366
Fat: 26 g
Protein: 31 g
Carbs: 2 g
Fiber: 1 g
Sugar: 0 g
Sodium: 895 mg

206.Ginger and Green Onion Fish

Preparation Time: 15 Minutes
Cooking Time: 15 Minutes
Servings: 2

Ingredients:
Bean Sauce:

- 2 Tbsp. low-sodium soy sauce
- 1 Tbsp. rice wine
- 1 Tbsp. doubanjiang (Chinese black bean paste)
- 1 tsp. minced fresh ginger
- 1 clove garlic, minced

Vegetables and Fish:

- 1 Tbsp. peanut oil
- ¼ cup julienned green onions
- ¼ cup chopped fresh cilantro
- 2 Tbsp. julienned fresh ginger
- 2 (6 oz./170 g) white fish fillets, such as tilapia

Directions:
For the sauce:

1. In a small bowl, combine all the ingredients and stir until well combined; set aside.

For the vegetables and fish:

1. In a medium bowl, combine the peanut oil, green onions, cilantro, and ginger. Toss to combine.
2. Cut two squares of parchment large enough to hold one fillet and half of the vegetables. Place one fillet on each parchment square, top with the vegetables, and pour over the sauce. Bend over the parchment paper and tuck the sides in small, tight folds to hold the fish, vegetables, and sauce securely inside the packet.
3. Place the packets in a single layer in the air fryer basket. Roast at 350°F (177°C) for 15 minutes.
4. Transfer each packet to a dinner plate. Cut open with scissors just before serving.

Nutrition:
Calories: 237
Fat: 9 g
Protein: 36 g
Carbs: 3 g
Fiber: 0 g
Sugar: 0 g
Sodium: 641 mg

207.Asian Sesame Cod

Preparation Time: 5 Minutes
Cooking Time: 7 to 9 Minutes
Servings: 1

Ingredients:

- 1 Tbsp. reduced-sodium soy sauce
- 2 tsp. honey
- 1 tsp. sesame seeds
- 6 oz. (170 g) cod fillet

Directions:

1. In a small bowl, combine the soy sauce and honey.
2. Spray the air fryer basket with nonstick cooking spray, then place the cod in the basket, brush with the soy mixture, and sprinkle sesame seeds on top. Roast at 360°F (182°C) for 7 to 9 minutes or until opaque.
3. Remove the fish and cool on a wire rack for 5 minutes before serving.

Nutrition:
Calories: 141
Fat: 1 g
Protein: 26 g
Carbs: 7 g
Fiber: 1 g
Sugar: 6 g
Sodium: 466 mg

208.Lemon Scallops with Asparagus

Preparation Time: 10 Minutes
Cooking Time: 7 to 10 Minutes
Servings: 4

Ingredients:

- ½ lb. (227 g) asparagus, ends trimmed and cut into 2-inch pieces
- 1 cup sugar snap peas
- 1 lb. (454 g) sea scallops
- 1 Tbsp. lemon juice
- 2 tsp. olive oil
- ½ tsp. dried thyme
- Pinch salt
- Freshly ground black pepper, to taste

Directions:

1. Place the asparagus and sugar snap peas in the air fryer basket. Air fry at 400°F (204°C) for 2 to 3 minutes or until the vegetables are just getting tender.
2. Meanwhile, check the scallops for a small muscle attached to the side, and pull it off and discard.
3. In a medium bowl, toss the scallops with lemon juice, olive oil, thyme, salt, and pepper. Place into the air fryer basket on top of the vegetables.
4. Air fry for 5 to 7 minutes, tossing the basket once during the cooking time until the scallops are just firm when tested with your finger and are opaque in the center, and the vegetables are tender. Serve immediately.

Nutrition:

Calories: 163
Fat: 4 g
Protein: 22 g
Carbs: 10 g
Fiber: 3 g
Sugar: 3 g
Sodium: 225 mg

209. Fish Tacos

Preparation Time: 15 Minutes
Cooking Time: 9 to 12 Minutes
Servings: 4

Ingredients:

- 1 lb. (454 g) white fish fillets, such as snapper
- 1 Tbsp. olive oil
- 3 Tbsp. freshly squeezed lemon juice, divided
- 1½ cups chopped red cabbage
- ½ cup salsa
- 1/3 cup sour cream
- 6 whole-wheat tortillas
- 2 avocados, peeled and chopped

Directions:

1. Spray the fish with olive oil and sprinkle with 1 Tbsp. of lemon juice. Place in the air fryer basket and air fry at 400°F (204°C) meant for 9 to 12 minutes or until the fish just flakes when tested with a fork.
2. Meanwhile, combine the remaining 2 Tbsp. of lemon juice, cabbage, salsa, and sour cream in a medium bowl.
3. When the fish is cooked, remove it from the air fryer basket and break it into large pieces.
4. Let everyone assemble their taco combining the fish, tortillas, cabbage mixture, and avocados.

Nutrition:

Calories: 547
Fat: 27 g
Protein: 33 g
Carbs: 43 g
Fiber: 12 g
Sugar: 4 g
Sodium: 679 mg

210. Spicy Cajun Shrimp

Preparation Time: 7 Minutes
Cooking Time: 10 to 13 Minutes
Servings: 2 cups

Ingredients:

- ½ lb. (227 g) shrimp, peeled and deveined
- 1 Tbsp. olive oil
- 1 tsp. ground cayenne pepper
- ½ tsp. Old Bay Seasoning
- ½ tsp. paprika
- 1/8 tsp salt
- ½ a lemon, juiced

Directions:

1. In a large bowl, place the shrimp, olive oil, cayenne pepper, Old Bay Seasoning, paprika, and salt; toss to combine.
2. Transfer to the air fryer basket and roast at 390°F (199°C) for 10 to 13 minutes, until browned.
3. Sprinkle a bit of lemon juice over the shrimp before serving.

Nutrition:

Calories: 159
Fat: 7 g
Protein: 23 g
Carbs: 1 g
Fiber: 0 g
Sugar: 0 g
Sodium: 291 mg

211. Garlic Parmesan Roasted Shrimp

Preparation Time: 7 Minutes
Cooking Time: 10 to 13 Minutes
Servings: 4 cups

Ingredients:

- 1 lb. (454 g) jumbo shrimp, peeled and deveined
- 1/3 cup Parmesan cheese
- 1 Tbsp. olive oil
- 1 tsp. onion powder
- 2 tsp. minced garlic
- ½ tsp. ground black pepper
- ¼ tsp. dried basil

Directions:

1. In a large bowl, toss to combine the shrimp, Parmesan cheese, olive oil, onion powder, garlic, pepper, and basil.

2. Transfer to the air fryer basket and roast at 350°F (177°C) for 10 to 13 minutes, until the shrimp are browned, and serve.

Nutrition:
Calories: 162
Fat: 6 g
Protein: 25 g
Carbs: 2 g
Fiber: 0 g
Sugar: 0 g
Sodium: 271 mg

212. Quick Shrimp Scampi

Preparation Time: 10 Minutes
Cooking Time: 7 to 8 Minutes
Servings: 2

Ingredients:

- 30 (1 lb./454 g) uncooked large shrimp, peeled, deveined, and tails removed
- 2 tsp. olive oil
- 1 garlic clove, thinly sliced
- ½ lemon, juice, and zest
- 1/8 tsp kosher salt
- Pinch red pepper flakes (optional)
- 1 Tbsp. chopped fresh parsley

Directions:

1. Spray a baking pan with nonstick cooking spray, then combine the shrimp, olive oil, sliced garlic, lemon juice and zest, kosher salt, and red pepper flakes (if using) in the pan, tossing to coat. Place in the air fryer basket.
2. Roast at 360°F (182°C) for 7 to 8 minutes or until firm and bright pink.
3. Remove the shrimp from the fryer, place it on a serving plate, and sprinkle the parsley on top. Serve warm.

Nutrition:
Calories: 321
Fat: 13 g
Protein: 46 g
Carbs: 5 g
Fiber: 0 g
Sugar: 1 g
Sodium: 383 mg

213. Mustard-Crusted Fish Fillets

Preparation Time: 5 Minutes
Cooking Time: 8 to 11 Minutes
Servings: 4

Ingredients:

- 5 tsp. low-sodium yellow mustard
- 1 Tbsp. freshly squeezed lemon juice
- 4 (3.5 oz.) sole fillets
- ½ tsp. dried thyme
- ½ tsp. dried marjoram
- 1/8 tsp freshly ground black pepper
- 1 slice low-sodium whole-wheat bread, crumbled
- 2 tsp. olive oil

Directions:

1. In a small bowl, stir the mustard and lemon juice together. Spread this evenly over the fillets. Place them in the air fryer basket, preheated to 360°F.
2. In another small bowl, mix the thyme, marjoram, pepper, bread crumbs, and olive oil. Mix until combined.
3. Gently but firmly, press the spice mixture onto each fish fillet's top.
4. Bake for 8 to 11 minutes, or until the fish reaches an internal temperature of at least 145°F on a meat thermometer and the topping is browned and crisp. Serve immediately.

Nutrition:
Calories: 142
Fat: 4 g (25% of calories from fat)
Saturated Fat: 1 g
Protein: 20 g
Carbohydrates: 5 g
Sodium: 140 g
Fiber: 1 g
Sugar: 1 g

214. Fish and Vegetable Tacos

Preparation Time: 15 Minutes
Cooking Time: 9 to 12 Minutes
Servings: 4

Ingredients:

- 1 lb. white fish fillets, such as sole or cod
- 2 tsp. olive oil
- 3 Tbsp. freshly squeezed lemon juice, divided
- 1 ½ cups chopped red cabbage
- 1 large carrot, grated
- ½ cup low-sodium salsa
- 1/3 cup low-fat Greek yogurt
- 4 soft low-sodium whole-wheat tortillas

Directions:

1. Spray the fish with olive oil and drizzle with 1 Tbsp. of lemon juice. Fry in the air fryer basket for 9 to 12 minutes at 360°, or till the fish just flakes when tested with a fork.
2. In the meantime, in a medium bowl, stir together the remaining 2 Tbsps. of lemon juice, the red cabbage, carrot, salsa, and yogurt.
3. When the fish is cooked, remove it from the air fryer basket and break it up into large pieces.

4. Fill each tortilla with fish and top with the vegetable salsa.

Nutrition:
Calories: 209
Fat: 3 g (13% of calories from fat)
Saturated Fat: 0 g
Protein: 18 g
Carbohydrates: 30 g
Sodium: 116 mg
Fiber: 1 g
Sugar: 4 g

215.Lighter Fish and Chips

Preparation Time: 10 Minutes
Cooking Time: 11 to 15 Minutes (Chips), 11 to 15 Minutes (Cod Fillets)
Servings: 4

Ingredients:

- 2 russet potatoes, peeled, thinly sliced, rinsed, and patted dry
- 1 egg white
- 1 Tbsp. freshly squeezed lemon juice
- 1/3 cup ground almonds
- 2 slices low-sodium whole-wheat bread, finely crumbled
- ½ tsp. dried basil
- 4 (4-oz.) cod fillets

Directions:

1. Preheat the air fryer to 360°F.
2. Put the potato slices in the air fryer basket and air-fry for 11 to 15 minutes, or until crisp and brown. With tongs, turn the fries twice during cooking.
3. In the meantime, in a shallow bowl, beat the egg white and lemon juice until frothy.
4. On a plate, mix the almonds, bread crumbs, and basil.
5. Dip the fillets into the egg white mixture and then into the almond–bread crumb mixture to coat. Place the coated fillets on a wire rack to dry while the fries cook.
6. When the potatoes are done, transfer them to a baking sheet and keep warm in the oven on low heat
7. Air-fry the fish in the air fryer basket for 10 to 14 minutes, or until the fish grasps an inner temperature of at least 140°F on a meat thermometer and the coating is browned and crisp. Serve immediately with the potatoes.

Nutrition:
Calories: 247
Fat: 5 g (18% of calories from fat)
Saturated Fat: 0 g
Protein: 27 g
Carbohydrates: 25 g
Sodium: 131 mg
Fiber: 3 g
Sugar: 3 g

Chapter 8. Desserts Recipes

N. 216 Vanilla Bread Pudding

N. 224 Simple Raspberry Mug Cake

N. 235 Coconut Balls

N. 238 Apple Doughnuts

N. 243 Coconut Cupcakes

N. 256 Walnut Carrot Cake

216.Vanilla Bread Pudding

Preparation Time: 10 minutes
Cooking Time: 20 minutes
Servings: 4

Ingredients:

- 3 eggs, lightly beaten
- 1 tsp. coconut oil
- 1 tsp. vanilla
- 4 cup bread cubes
- ½ tsp. cinnamon
- ¼ cup raisins
- ¼ cup chocolate chips
- 2 cups milk
- ¼ tsp. salt

Directions:

1. Preheat the air fryer to 320°F. Spray a baking pan with nonstick cooking spray.
2. Add bread cubes to a baking dish.
3. In a large bowl, mix the remaining ingredients.
4. Pour the bowl mixture into the baking dish on top of bread cubes and cover the dish with foil.
5. Place baking dish in the air fryer and bake for 20 minutes.
6. Remove the foil and bake for a further 5 minutes.
7. Carefully remove the baking dish from the air fryer.
8. Serve and enjoy.

Nutrition:
Calories: 230
Fat:10.1 g
Carbohydrates: 25 g
Sugar: 16.7 g
Protein: 9.2 g
Cholesterol: 135 mg

217.Blueberry Cupcakes

Preparation Time: 10 minutes
Cooking Time: 20 minutes
Servings: 6

Ingredients:

- 2 eggs, lightly beaten
- ¼ cup butter, softened
- ½ tsp. baking soda
- 1 tsp. baking powder
- 1 tsp. vanilla extract
- ½ fresh lemon juice
- 1 lemon zest
- ¼ cup sour cream
- ¼ cup milk
- 1 cup Splenda for baking
- ¾ cup fresh blueberries
- 1 cup all-purpose flour
- ¼ tsp. salt

Directions:

1. Preheat the air fryer to 320°F. Lightly grease a silicone cupcake pan with cooking spray.
2. Add all ingredients into the large bowl and mix well.
3. Pour batter into the silicone cupcake pan and place it in the air fryer oven. Bake for 20 minutes.
4. Once done, remove from the oven. Place the cupcakes on a wire rack to cool.
5. Serve and enjoy.

Nutrition:
Calories: 330
Fat: 11.6 g
Carbohydrates: 53.6 g
Sugar: 36 g
Protein: 4.9 g
Cholesterol: 80 mg

218.Moist Pumpkin Brownie

Preparation Time: 10 minutes
Cooking Time: 30 minutes
Servings: 4

Ingredients:

- 2 eggs, lightly beaten
- ¾ cup pumpkin puree
- ½ tsp. baking powder
- 1/3 cup cocoa powder
- ½ cup almond flour
- 1 Tbsp. vanilla
- ¼ cup milk
- 1 cup maple syrup

Directions:

1. Preheat the air fryer oven to 330°F.
2. Place all ingredients into a large bowl and mix until well combined.
3. Spray a spring-form pan with cooking spray.
4. Pour batter into the pan and cover the pan with foil.
5. Put the cake pan in the air fryer and bake covered for 20 minutes. Remove the foil and bake for a further 5 minutes.
6. Once done, remove cake from the oven and let it rest on a wire rack for 10 minutes.
7. Remove the spring-form pan. Once cooled, slice and serve.

Nutrition:
Calories: 306
Fat: 5.5 g
Carbohydrates: 62.9 g
Sugar: 49.9 g

Protein: 5.8 g
Cholesterol: 83 mg

219.Mini Choco Cake

Preparation Time: 10 minutes
Cooking Time: 15 minutes
Servings: 2

Ingredients:

- 2 eggs
- 2 Tbsp. swerve
- ¼ cup cocoa powder
- ½ tsp. vanilla
- ½ tsp. baking powder
- 2 Tbsp. heavy cream

Directions:

1. Preheat the air fryer oven to 330°F.
2. In a bowl, blend all dry ingredients until combined.
3. Add all wet ingredients to the dry mixture and whisk until smooth.
4. Spray 2 ramekins with cooking spray.
5. Pour batter into the ramekins.
6. Place the ramekins in the air fryer oven and bake for 15 or until done.
7. Carefully remove the ramekins from the pot and let it cool.
8. Serve and enjoy.

Nutrition:
Calories: 143
Fat: 11.3 g
Carbohydrates: 22.4 g
Sugar: 15.7 g
Protein: 7.8 g
Cholesterol: 184 mg

220. Cinnamon Pears

Preparation Time: 10 minutes
Cooking Time: 12 minutes
Servings: 4

Ingredients:

- 4 firm pears, peeled
- ½ tsp. nutmeg
- 1/3 cup splenda, or all-purpose sugar substitute blend
- 1 tsp. ginger
- 4 whole cloves.
- 1 cinnamon stick
- 1 cup orange juice

Directions:

1. Preheat the air fryer oven to 330°F.
2. Add orange juice and all spices into a small pot. Bring to a boil, reduce heat and simmer for 5 minutes. Remove from heat and set aside.
3. Place the pears in the air fryer basket and bake for 6 to 7 minutes.
4. Carefully remove pears from the air fryer and set them aside.
5. Discard cinnamon sticks and cloves from the sauce pot.
6. Add sugar substitiute to the pot and cook the sauce until thickened.
7. Pour the sauce over pears and serve.

Nutrition:
Calories: 221
Fat: 0.6 g
Carbohydrates: 57.5 g
Sugar: 42.4 g
Protein: 1.3 g
Cholesterol: 0 mg

221.Delicious Pumpkin Pudding

Preparation Time: 10 minutes
Cooking Time: 25 minutes
Servings: 6

Ingredients:

- 2 large eggs, lightly beaten
- ½ cup milk
- ½ tsp. vanilla
- 1 tsp. pumpkin pie spice
- 14 oz. pumpkin puree
- ¾ cup swerve

Directions:

1. Preheat the air fryer oven to 330°F.
2. Spray a baking dish with cooking spray and set it aside.
3. In a large bowl, whisk eggs with the remaining ingredients.
4. Pour the mixture into the prepared dish and cover with foil.
5. Place dish in the air fryer and bake for 20 minutes.
6. Remove the foil and bake for a further 5 minutes.
7. As soon as it is done, carefully remove the dish from the air fryer and let it cool.
8. Place pudding dish in the refrigerator for 7–8 hours.
9. Serve and enjoy.

Nutrition:
Calories: 58
Fat: 2.3 g
Carbohydrates: 36.7 g
Sugar: 33.3 g
Protein: 3.5 g
Cholesterol: 64 mg

222. Saffron Rice Pudding

Preparation Time: 10 minutes
Cooking Time: 15 minutes
Servings: 6

Ingredients:

- ½ cup rice
- ½ tsp. cardamom powder
- 4 cups milk
- ½ cup all-purpose sugar substitue blend
- 2 Tbsp. shredded coconut
- 1 tsp. saffron
- 3 Tbsp. raisins
- 1 Tbsp. ghee
- 1/8 tsp. salt
- ½ cup water

Directions:

1. Preheat the air fryer oven to 250°F.
2. Add ghee to an air fryer pan.
3. Add rice and cook for 1 minute.
4. Add 3 cups milk, coconut, raisins, saffron, nuts, cardamom powder, sugar, ½ cup water, and salt, and mix well.
5. Close the air fryer, increase the heat to 325°F and bake the pudding for 15 minutes.
6. Add remaining milk and stir well; bake for a further 5 minutes.
7. Serve and enjoy.

Nutrition:
Calories: 280
Fat: 9.9 g
Carbohydrates: 42.1 g
Sugar: 27 g
Protein: 8.2 g
Cholesterol: 19 mg

223. Yogurt Custard

Preparation Time: 10 minutes
Cooking Time: 20 minutes
Servings: 6

Ingredients:

- 1 cup plain yogurt
- 1 ½ tsp. ground cardamom
- 1 cup keto sweetened condensed milk
- 1 cup milk

Directions:

1. Preheat the air fryer oven to 250°F.
2. Add all ingredients into the heat-safe bowl and stir to combine.
3. Cover the bowl with foil.
4. Place the bowl in the air fryer and cook for 15 minutes.
5. Remove the foil and bake for a further 5 minutes.
6. Once done, remove the custard from the air fryer and let it cool.
7. Once the custard bowl is cool, place it in the refrigerator for 1 hour.
8. Serve and enjoy.

Nutrition:
Calories: 215
Fat: 5.8 g
Carbohydrates: 33 g
Sugar: 32.4 g
Protein: 7.7 g
Cholesterol: 23 mg

224. Simple Raspberry Mug Cake

Preparation Time: 10 minutes
Cooking Time: 12 to 13 minutes
Servings: 3

Ingredients:

- 3 eggs
- 1 cup almond flour
- ½ tsp. vanilla
- 1 Tbsp. swerve
- 2 Tbsp. chocolate chips
- ½ cup raspberries
- Pinch of salt

Directions:

1. Preheat the air fryer oven to 220°F.
2. Add all ingredients into a large bowl and mix until well combined.
3. Pour batter into greased heat-safe mugs. Cover with foil and place in the air fryer.
4. Close the air fryer and cook for 10 minutes. Remove the foil and cook for a further 2 to 3 minutes.
5. Once done, remove from the air fryer and let it cool to room temperature.
6. Serve and enjoy.

Nutrition:
Calories: 326
Fat: 25.3 g
Carbohydrates: 20 g
Sugar: 11.3 g
Protein: 11.3 g
Cholesterol: 165 mg

225. Chocolate Mousse

Preparation Time: 10 minutes
Cooking Time: 6 minutes
Servings: 5

Ingredients:

- 4 egg yolks
- ¼ cup water
- ½ cup all-purpose sugar substitiute blend
- 1 tsp. vanilla
- 1 cup heavy cream
- ½ cup cocoa powder
- ½ cup milk
- ¼ tsp. sea salt

Directions:

1. Preheat the air fryer oven to 200°F.
2. Whisk egg yolks in a bowl until fluffy.
3. In a saucepan, add cocoa, water, and sugar, and whisk over medium heat until sugar is melted.
4. Add milk and cream to the saucepan and whisk to combine. Do not boil.
5. Add vanilla and salt; stir well.
6. Pour mixture into ramekins and place in the air fryer.
7. Close the air fryer and cook for 6 minutes.
8. Once done, remove from the air fryer and place it in the refrigerator for 2 to 3 hours until set.
9. Serve and enjoy.

Nutrition:
Calories: 235
Fat: 14.1 g
Carbohydrates: 27.2 g
Sugar: 21.5 g
Protein: 5 g
Cholesterol: 203 mg

226. Cardamom Zucchini Pudding

Preparation Time: 10 minutes
Cooking Time: 10 minutes
Servings: 4

Ingredients:

- 1 ¾ cups zucchini, shredded
- 5 oz. half and half
- 5.5 oz. milk
- 1 tsp. cardamom powder
- 1/3 cup Swerve

Directions:

1. Preheat the air fryer oven to 250°F.
9. Add all ingredients except cardamom into a heat-safe bowl and stir to combine.
2. Place the bowl in the air fryer and cook for 10 minutes.
3. As soon as done, remove from the air fryer.
4. Stir in cardamom and serve.

Nutrition:
Calories: 138
Fat: 5 g
Carbohydrates: 22.1 g
Sugar: 19.4 g
Protein: 3 g
Cholesterol: 16 mg

227. Yummy Strawberry Cobbler

Preparation Time: 10 minutes
Cooking Time: 12 minutes
Servings: 3

Ingredients:

- 1 cup strawberries, sliced
- ½ tsp. vanilla
- 1/3 cup butter
- 1 cup milk
- 1 tsp. baking powder
- ½ cup all-purpose sugar substitute blend
- 1 ¼ cups all-purpose flour

Directions:

1. Preheat the air fryer oven to 250°F.
2. In a large bowl, add all ingredients except strawberries and stir to combine.
3. Add sliced strawberries and fold in.
4. Grease ramekins with cooking spray, then pour batter into the ramekins.
5. Place ramekins in the air fryer and cook for 12 minutes.
6. Serve and enjoy.

Nutrition:
Calories: 555
Fat: 22.8 g
Carbohydrates: 81.7 g
Sugar: 39.6 g
Protein: 8.6 g
Cholesterol: 61 mg

228. Peach Cobbler

Preparation Time: 10 minutes
Cooking Time: 20 minutes
Servings: 6

Ingredients:

- 20 oz. can low-sugar peach pie filling
- 1 ½ tsp. cinnamon
- ¼ tsp nutmeg
- 14.5 oz. keto vanilla cake mix
- ½ cup butter, melted

Directions:

1. Preheat the air fryer oven to 250°F.
2. Add peach pie filling into a greased air fryer pan.

3. In a large bowl, mix the remaining ingredients and spread it over peach pie filling.
4. Close the air fryer and bake for 15 minutes or until a toothpick inserted in the middle comes out clean
5. Serve and enjoy.

Nutrition:
Calories: 445
Fat: 15.4 g
Carbohydrates: 76.1 g
Sugar: 47.7 g
Protein: 0.2 g
Cholesterol: 41 mg

229. Vanilla Peanut Butter Fudge

Preparation Time: 10 minutes
Cooking Time: 30 minutes
Servings: 12

Ingredients:

- 1 cup sugar-free chocolate chips
- 8.5 oz. cream cheese
- ¼ cup peanut butter
- ½ tsp. vanilla
- ¼ cup swerve

Directions:

1. Preheat the air fryer oven to 100°F.
2. Add all ingredients into a heat-safe bowl and stir to combine.
3. Place in the air fryer and cook for 20 minutes.
4. Stir until smooth and cook for 10 minutes more.
5. Pour mixture into a baking pan and place in the fridge until set.
6. Slice and serve.

Nutrition:
Calories: 177
Fat: 13.9 g
Carbohydrates: 14.9 g
Sugar: 12.8 g
Protein: 3.9 g
Cholesterol: 25 mg

230. Fruity Oreo Muffins

Preparation Time: 15 minutes
Cooking Time: 10 minutes
Servings: 6

Ingredients:

- 1 cup milk
- 1 pack sugar-free chocolate sandwich cookies, crushed
- ¾ tsp. baking powder
- 1 banana, peeled and chopped
- 1 apple, peeled, cored and chopped
- 1 tsp. cocoa powder
- 1 tsp. honey
- 1 tsp. fresh lemon juice
- A pinch of ground cinnamon

Directions:

1. Preheat the air fryer to 320°F and grease 6 muffin cups lightly.
2. Mix milk, biscuits, cocoa powder, baking soda, and baking powder in a bowl until well combined.
3. Transfer the mixture into the muffin cups and cook for about 10 minutes.
4. Remove from the air fryer and place the muffin cups on a wire rack to cool.
5. Meanwhile, mix the banana, apple, honey, lemon juice, and cinnamon in another bowl.
6. Scoop some portion of muffins from the center and fill with the fruit mixture to serve.

Nutrition:
Calories: 182
Fat: 3.1g
Carbohydrates: 31.4g
Sugar: 19.5g
Protein: 3.1g
Sodium: 196mg

231. Chocolate Mug Cake

Preparation Time: 15 minutes
Cooking Time: 13 minutes
Servings: 1

Ingredients:

- ¼ cup self-rising flour
- 1 Tbsp. cocoa powder
- 3 Tbsps. whole milk
- 5 Tbsps. caster sugar
- 3 Tbsps. coconut oil

Directions:

1. Preheat the Air fryer to 390°F and grease a large mug lightly.
2. Mix all the ingredients in a shallow mug until well combined.
3. Arrange the mug into the Air fryer basket and cook for about 13 minutes.
4. Dish out and serve warm.

Nutrition:
Calories: 729
Fat: 43.3g
Carbohydrates: 88.8g
Sugar: 62.2g
Protein: 5.7g
Sodium: 20mg

232. Dark Chocolate Cheesecake

Preparation Time: 20 minutes
Cooking Time: 34 minutes
Servings: 6
Ingredients:

- 3 eggs, whites and yolks separated
- 1 cup dark chocolate, chopped
- ½ cup cream cheese, softened
- 2 Tbsps. cocoa powder
- ¼ cup date jam
- 2 Tbsps. powdered sugar (optional)

Directions:

1. Preheat the air fryer to 285°F and grease a cake pan lightly.
2. Refrigerate egg whites in a bowl to chill before using.
3. Microwave chocolate and cream cheese on high for about 3 minutes.
4. Remove from microwave and whisk in the egg yolks.
5. Whisk together egg whites until firm peaks form and combine with the chocolate mixture.
6. Transfer the mixture into a cake pan and arrange in the air fryer basket.
7. Cook for about 30 minutes and dish out.
8. Dust with powdered sugar and spread dates jam on top to serve.

Nutrition:
Calories: 298
Fat: 18.3g
Carbohydrates: 29.7g
Sugar: 24.5g
Protein: 6.3g
Sodium: 119mg

233. Chocolate Cookies

Preparation time: 10 minutes
Cooking time: 7 minutes
Servings: 4
Ingredients:

- 4 Tbsps. almond flour
- 1 Tbsp. ground oatmeal
- 2 Tbsps. coconut milk
- 2 Tbsps. Erythritol
- 2 Tbsps. cocoa powder
- 1 oz. sugar-free chocolate chips
- ½ tsp. vanilla extract
- 2 Tbsps. coconut oil
- ¾ tsp. ground cardamom

Directions:

1. In a mixing bowl combine all ingredients and knead to form a soft and non-sticky dough.
2. Then make a log from the dough and cut it into equal pieces.
3. Make balls from the dough.
4. Line the air fryer with baking paper and insert the dough balls inside.
5. Cook the cookies for 7 minutes at 350°F.

Nutrition:
Calories 164
Fat 9.6
Fiber 1.4
Carbs 19.1
Protein 2.2

234. Egg Clouds

Preparation time: 10 minutes
Cooking time: 45 minutes
Servings: 6
Ingredients:

- 2 egg whites
- ½ cup Erythritol
- 1 tsp. lemon juice

Directions:

1. Whisk the egg whites till it forms soft peaks.
2. Then add Erythritol and lemon juice and whisk the egg whites till you get the stiff peaks.
3. Line the air fryer basket with parchment.
4. With the help of the spoon or a pastry bag, make small meringues on the parchment.
5. Cook the "clouds" at 310°F for 45 minutes.

Nutrition:
Calories 68
Fat 0
Fiber 0
Carbs 16.8
Protein 1.2

235. Coconut Balls

Preparation time: 10 minutes
Cooking time: 40 minutes
Servings: 4
Ingredients:

- 1 egg white
- 4 Tbsps. coconut flakes
- 2 Tbsps. Erythritol

Directions:

1. Mix together egg white and Erythritol and whisk to firm peaks.
2. After this, slowly add coconut flakes and stir the mixture.
3. Line the air fryer basket with baking paper.
4. With the help of the spoon make "clouds" and place them in the air fryer or make them directly in the air fryer.
5. Cook the coconut clouds for 40 minutes at 330°F or until the "clouds" are light brown.

Nutrition:
Calories 44, fat 1.7, fiber 0.5, carbs 6.8, protein 1.1

236.Almond Cookies

Preparation time: 30 minutes
Cooking time: 30 minutes
Servings: 12
Ingredients:

- 9 oz. almond flour
- 1 tsp. vanilla extract
- 1 egg, beaten
- 2 Tbsps. coconut oil, softened
- ½ tsp. ground cardamom
- 2 Tbsps. Erythritol

Directions:

1. Add vanilla extract, coconut oil, ground cardamom, and Erythritol to the almond flour.
2. Add egg and knead the dough.
3. Make 12 balls from the dough. Refrigerate them for 20 minutes.
4. Make crosses on the surface of the cookie with a fork.
5. Place the cookies in the air fryer and cook the cookies for 15 minutes at 350°F.
6. Repeat the same steps with the remaining dough balls.

Nutrition:
Calories 106
Fat 3
Fiber 1.9
Carbs 17.3
Protein 3.1

237.Cream Doughnuts

Preparation Time: 15 minutes
Cooking Time: 16 minutes
Servings: 8
Ingredients:

- 4 Tbsps. butter, softened and divided
- 2 egg yolks
- 2¼ cups plain flour
- 1½ tsps. baking powder
- ½ cup Swerve
- 1 tsp. salt
- ½ cup sour cream
- ½ cup heavy cream

Directions:

1. Preheat the air fryer to 355°F and grease an air fryer basket lightly.
2. Sift together flour, baking powder and salt in a large bowl.
3. Combine sugar and cold butter and mix until a coarse crumbs are formed.
4. Stir in the egg yolks, ½ of the sour cream and 1/3 of the flour mixture and mix until a dough is formed.
5. Add remaining sour cream and 1/3 of the flour mixture and mix until well combined.
6. Stir in the remaining flour mixture and combine well.
7. Roll the dough into ½ inch thickness on a floured surface and cut into donuts with a donut cutter.
8. Coat butter on both sides of the donuts and arrange in the air fryer basket.
9. Cook for about 8 minutes until golden, and top with heavy cream to serve.

Nutrition:
Calories: 297
Fats: 13g
Carbohydrates: 40.7g
Sugar: 12.6g
Proteins: 5g
Sodium: 346mg

238.Apple Doughnuts

Preparation Time: 20 minutes
Cooking Time: 5 minutes
Servings: 6
Ingredients:

- 2½ cups plus 2 Tbsps. all-purpose flour
- 1½ tsps. baking powder
- 2 Tbsps. unsalted butter, softened
- 1 egg
- ½ pink lady apple, peeled, cored and grated
- 1 cup apple cider
- ½ tsp. ground cinnamon
- ½ tsp. salt
- ½ cup brown sugar substitute

Directions:

1. Preheat the air fryer to 360°F and grease an air fryer basket lightly.
2. Bring the apple cider to a boil in a medium pan over medium-high heat and then reduce the heat.
3. Let it simmer for about 15 minutes and transfer to a bowl.
4. Sift together flour, baking powder, baking soda, cinnamon, and salt in a large bowl.
5. Mix the brown sugar, egg, cooled apple cider and butter in another bowl.
6. Stir in the flour mixture and grated apple and mix to form a dough.
7. Wrap the dough with plastic wrap and refrigerate for about 30 minutes.
8. Roll the dough into 1-inch thickness and cut the doughnuts with a doughnut cutter.
9. Arrange the doughnuts into the air fryer basket and cook for about 5 minutes, flipping once in between.
10. Serve warm.

Nutrition:
Calories: 433
Fat: 11g
Carbohydrates: 78.3g
Sugar: 35g
Protein: 6.8g
Sodium: 383mg

239.Doughnuts Pudding

Preparation Time: 15 minutes
Cooking Time: 1 hour
Servings 4
Ingredients:

- 6 sugar-free "glazed" doughnuts, cut into small pieces
- ¾ cup frozen sweet cherries
- ½ cup raisins
- ½ cup sugar-free chocolate chips
- 4 egg yolks
- ¼ cup Swerve
- 1 tsp. ground cinnamon
- 1½ cups whipping cream

Directions:

1. Preheat the air fryer to 310°F and grease a baking dish lightly.
2. Mix doughnut pieces, cherries, raisins, chocolate chips, sugar, and cinnamon in a large bowl.
3. Whisk the egg yolks with whipping cream in another bowl until well combined.
4. Combine the egg yolk mixture into the doughnut mixture and mix well.
5. Arrange the doughnuts mixture evenly into the baking dish and transfer into the air fryer basket.
6. Cook for about 60 minutes and dish out to serve warm.

Nutrition:
Calories: 786
Fat: 43.2g
Carbohydrates: 9.3g
Sugar: 60.7g
Protein: 11g
Sodium: 419mg

240.Chocolate Soufflé

Preparation Time: 15 minutes
Cooking Time: 16 minutes
Servings: 2
Ingredients:

- 3 ounces sugar-free chocolate, chopped
- ¼ cup butter
- 2 eggs, egg yolks and whites separated
- 2 Tbsps. all-purpose flour
- 3 Tbsps. All-purpose sugar substitute blend
- ½ tsp. pure vanilla extract
- 1 tsp. powdered sugar, plus extra for dusting (optional)

Directions:

1. Preheat the air fryer to 330°F and grease 2 ramekins lightly.
2. Microwave butter and chocolate on high heat for about 2 minutes until melted.
3. Whisk the egg yolks, sugar, and vanilla extract in a bowl.
4. Add the chocolate mixture and flour and mix until well combined.
5. Whisk the egg whites in another bowl until soft peaks form and fold into the chocolate mixture.
6. Sprinkle each ramekin with a pinch of sugar and transfer the mixture into the ramekins.
7. Arrange the ramekins into the air fryer basket and cook for about 14 minutes.
8. Dish out and serve sprinkled with the powdered sugar to serve.

Nutrition:
Calories: 569
Fat: 38.8g
Carbohydrates: 54.1g
Sugar: 42.2g
Protein: 6.9g
Sodium: 225mg

241.Crustless Cheesecake

Preparation Time: 5 minutes
Cooking Time: 10 minutes
Servings: 2
Ingredients:

- 16 ounces cream cheese, reduced-fat, softened
- 2 Tbsps. sour cream, reduced-fat
- 3/4 cup erythritol sweetener
- 1 tsp. vanilla extract, unsweetened
- 2 eggs
- 1/2 tsp. lemon juice

Directions:

1. Switch on the air fryer, insert fryer basket, grease it with olive oil, then shut with its lid, set the fryer at 350°F and preheat for 5 minutes.
2. Meanwhile, take two 4 inches spring-form pans, grease them with oil and set aside.
3. Crack the eggs in a bowl and then whisk in lemon juice, sweetener and vanilla until smooth.
4. Whisk in cream cheese and sour cream until blended and then divide the mixture evenly between prepared pans.
5. Open the fryer, place pans in it, close with its lid and cook for 10 minutes until cakes are set and inserted skewer into the cakes slide out clean.

6. When air fryer beeps, open its lid, take out the cake pans and let the cakes cool in them.
7. Take out the cakes from the pans, refrigerate for 3 hours until cooled and then serve.

Nutrition:
Calories: 318
Carbohydrates: 1 g
Fat: 29.7 g
Protein: 11.7 g
Fiber: 0 g

242. Mini Apple Oat Muffins

Preparation Time: 5minutes
Cooking Time: 25 minutes
Servings: 24

Ingredients:

- 1 ½ cups oats, old-fashioned
- 1 tsp. baking powder
- ½ tsp. cinnamon, ground
- ¼ tsp. baking soda
- ¼ tsp. salt
- ½ cup applesauce, unsweetened
- 3 Tbsps. canola oil
- 3 Tbsps. water
- 1 tsp. vanilla extract
- ½ cup almonds, slivered

Directions:

1. Preheat the air fryer to 350°F and grease a mini muffin pan.
2. Place the oats in a food processor and pulse into a fine flour.
3. Add the baking powder, cinnamon, baking soda, and salt.
4. Pulse until well combined, then add the applesauce, canola oil, water, and vanilla then blend until smooth.
5. Fold in the almonds and spoon the mixture into the muffin pan.
6. Bake for 22 to 25 minutes until a knife inserted in the center comes out clean.
7. Cool the muffins for 5 minutes, then turn out onto a wire rack.

Nutrition:
Calories: 70
Fat: 0.7 g
Carbohydrates: 14.7 g
Protein: 2.1 g
Fiber: 2.5 g

243. Coconut Cupcakes

Preparation Time: 10 minutes
Cooking Time: 30 minutes
Servings: 6

Ingredients:

- ½ cup butter
- ½ tsp. salt
- ¾ cup erythritol
- 1 cup almond milk, unsweetened
- 1 cup coconut flour
- 1 Tbsp. baking powder
- 3 tsps. vanilla extract
- 7 large eggs, beaten

Directions:

1. Preheat the air fryer to 350°F for 5 minutes.
2. Mix all ingredients using a hand mixer.
3. Pour into cupcake molds.
4. Place in the air fryer basket.
5. Bake for 30 minutes at 350°F or until a toothpick inserted in the middle comes out clean.
6. Bake by batches if necessary.
7. Allow to chill before serving.

Nutrition:
Calories: 235
Carbohydrates: 7.4g
Protein: 3.8g
Fat: 21.1g

244. Easy Baked Chocolate Mug Cake

Preparation Time: 10 minutes
Cooking Time: 15 minutes
Servings: 3

Ingredients:

- ½ cup cocoa powder
- ½ cup stevia powder
- 1 cup coconut cream
- 1 package cream cheese, room temperature
- 1 Tbsp. vanilla extract
- 4 Tbsps. butter

Directions:

1. Preheat the air fryer to 350°F for 5 minutes.
2. In a mixing bowl, combine all ingredients.
3. Use a hand mixer to mix everything until fluffy.
4. Pour into greased mugs.
5. Place the mugs in the fryer basket.
6. Bake for 15 minutes at 350°F.
7. Place in the fridge to chill before serving.

Nutrition:
Calories: 744
Carbohydrates: 15.3 g
Protein: 13.9g
Fat: 69.7g

245. Keto-Friendly Doughnut Recipe

Preparation Time: 10 minutes
Cooking Time: 20 minutes
Servings: 3
Ingredients:

- ¼ cup coconut milk
- ¼ cup erythritol
- ¼ cup flaxseed meal
- ¾ cup almond flour
- 1 Tbsp. cocoa powder
- 1 tsp. vanilla extract
- 2 large eggs, beaten
- 3 Tbsps. coconut oil

Directions:

1. Place all ingredients in a mixing bowl. Mix until well combined.
2. Scoop the dough into individual doughnut molds.
3. Preheat the air fryer for 5 minutes.
4. Cook for 20 minutes at 350°F.
5. Bake in batches if possible.

Nutrition:
Calories: 222
Carbohydrates: 5.1g
Protein: 3.9g
Fat: 20.7g

246. Zucchini-Choco Bread

Preparation Time: 10 minutes
Cooking Time: 20 minutes
Servings: 3
Ingredients:

- ¼ tsp. salt
- ½ cup almond milk
- ½ cup maple syrup
- ½ cup sunflower oil
- ½ cup unsweetened cocoa powder
- 1 cup oat flour
- 1 cup zucchini, shredded and squeezed
- 1 Tbsp. flax egg: (1 Tbsp. flax meal + 3 Tbsps. water)
- 1 tsp. apple cider vinegar
- 1 tsp. baking soda
- 1 tsp. vanilla extract
- 1/3 cup chocolate chips

Directions:

1. Preheat the air fryer to 350°F.
2. Line a baking dish that will fit the air fryer with parchment paper.
3. In a bowl, combine the flax meal, zucchini, sunflower oil, maple, vanilla, apple cider vinegar and milk.
4. Stir in the oat flour, baking soda, cocoa powder, and salt. Mix until well combined.
5. Add the chocolate chips.
6. Pour into the baking dish and cook for 15 minutes or until a toothpick inserted in the middle comes out clean.

Nutrition:
Calories: 213
Carbohydrates: 24.2 g
Protein: 4.6g
Fat. 10.9g

247. Apple-Toffee Upside-Down Cake

Preparation Time: 10 minutes
Cooking Time: 30 minutes
Servings: 3
Ingredients:

- ¼ cup almond butter
- ¼ cup sunflower oil
- ½ cup walnuts, chopped
- ¾ cup + 3 Tbsps. coconut sugar
- ¾ cup water
- 1 ½ tsps. mixed spice
- 1 cup plain flour
- 1 lemon, zest
- 1 tsp. baking soda
- 1 tsp. vinegar
- 3 baking apples, cored and sliced

Directions:

1. Preheat the air fryer to 390°F.
2. In a skillet, melt the almond butter and 3 tablespoons sugar. Pour the mixture into a baking dish that will fit in the air fryer. Arrange the slices of apples on top. Set aside.
3. In a mixing bowl, combine flour, ¾ cup sugar, and baking soda. Add the mixed spice.
4. In another bowl, mix the oil, water, vinegar, and lemon zest. Stir in the chopped walnuts.
5. Combine the wet ingredients to the dry ingredients until well combined.
6. Pour over the tin with apple slices.
7. Bake for 30 minutes or until a toothpick inserted comes out clean.

Nutrition:
Calories: 335
Carbohydrates: 39.6g
Protein: 3.8g
Fat: 17.9g

248. Cherry-Choco Bars

Preparation Time: 10 minutes
Cooking Time: 15 minutes
Servings: 3

Ingredients:

- ¼ tsp. salt
- ½ cup almonds, chopped
- ½ cup chia seeds
- ½ cup dark chocolate, chopped
- ½ cup dried cherries, chopped
- ½ cup prunes, pureed
- ½ cup quinoa, cooked
- ¾ cup almond butter
- 1/3 cup honey
- 2 cups old-fashioned oats
- 2 Tbsps. coconut oil

Directions:

1. Preheat the air fryer to 375°F.
2. In a mixing bowl, combine the oats, quinoa, chia seeds, almond, cherries, and chocolate.
3. In a saucepan, heat the almond butter, honey, and coconut oil.
4. Pour the butter mixture over the dry mixture. Add salt and prunes.
5. Mix until well combined.
6. Pour over a baking dish that can fit inside the air fryer.
7. Cook for 15 minutes.
8. Let it cool for an hour before slicing into bars.

Nutrition:

Calories: 321
Carbohydrates: 35g
Protein: 7g
Fat: 17g

249. Maple Cinnamon Buns

Preparation Time: 10 minutes
Cooking Time: 30 minutes
Servings: 3

Ingredients:

- ¼ cup icing sugar
- ½ cup pecan nuts, toasted, chopped
- ¾ cup Tbsp. unsweetened almond milk
- 1 ½ cup plain white flour, sifted
- 1 ½ Tbsps. active yeast
- 1 cup wholegrain flour, sifted
- 1 Tbsp. coconut oil, melted
- 1 Tbsp. ground flaxseed
- 2 ripe bananas, sliced
- 2 tsps. cinnamon powder
- 4 Medjool dates, pitted and chopped
- 4 Tbsps. maple syrup

Directions:

1. Heat the ¾ cup almond milk to lukewarm and add the maple syrup and yeast. Allow the yeast to activate for 5 to 10 minutes.
2. Meanwhile, mix together flaxseed and 3 tablespoons of water to make the egg replacement. Allow flaxseed to soak for 2 minutes. Add the coconut oil.
3. Pour the flaxseed mixture to the yeast mixture.
4. In another bowl, combine the two types of flour and the 1 tablespoon cinnamon powder. Add the yeast-flaxseed mixture and combine until dough forms.
5. Knead the dough on a floured surface for at least 10 minutes.
6. Place the kneaded dough in a greased bowl and cover with a kitchen towel. Leave in a warm and dark area for the bread to rise for 1 hour.
7. While the dough is rising, make the filling by mixing together the pecans, banana slices, and dates. Add 1 tablespoon of cinnamon powder.
8. Preheat the air fryer to 390°F.
9. Roll the risen dough on a floured surface until it is thin. Spread the pecan mixture on to the dough.
10. Roll up the dough and cut into nine slices.
11. Place inside a dish that will fit in the air fryer and cook for 30 minutes.
12. Once cooked, sprinkle with icing sugar.

Nutrition:

Calories: 293
Carbohydrates: 44.9g
Protein: 5.6g
Fat: 10.1 g

250. Yummy Banana Cookies

Preparation Time: 10 minutes
Cooking Time: 10 minutes
Servings: 6

Ingredients:

- 1 cup dates, pitted and chopped
- 1 tsp. vanilla
- 1/3 cup vegetable oil
- 2 cups rolled oats
- 4 ripe bananas

Directions:

1. Preheat the air fryer to 350°F.
2. In a bowl, mash the bananas and add in the rest of the ingredients.
3. Let it rest inside the fridge for 10 minutes.
4. Drop teaspoonful of mixture on cut parchment paper.
5. Place the cookies on parchment paper inside the air fryer basket. Make sure that the cookies do not overlap.
6. Cook for 20 minutes or until the edges are crispy.
7. Serve with almond milk.

Nutrition:

Calories: 382
Carbohydrates: 50.14g

Protein: 6.54g
Fat: 17.2g

251. Coffee Flavored Doughnuts

Preparation Time: 10 minutes
Cooking Time: 6 minutes
Servings: 6

Ingredients:

- ¼ cup coconut sugar
- ¼ cup coffee
- ½ tsp. salt
- 1 cup white all-purpose flour
- 1 Tbsp. sunflower oil
- 1 tsp. baking powder
- 2 Tbsps. aquafaba

Directions:

1. In a mixing bowl mix together the dry ingredients flour, sugar, salt, and baking powder.
2. In another bowl, combine the aquafaba, sunflower oil, and coffee.
3. Mix to form a dough.
4. Let the dough rest inside the fridge for 30 minutes.
5. Preheat the air fryer to 400°F.
6. Knead the dough and create doughnuts.
7. Arrange inside the air fryer in a single layer and cook for 6 minutes.
8. Do not shake so that the donut maintains its shape.

Nutrition:

Calories: 113
Carbohydrates: 20.45g
Protein: 2.16g
Fat: 2.54g

252. Crisped 'n Chewy Chonut Holes

Preparation Time: 10 minutes
Cooking Time: 10 minutes
Servings: 6

Ingredients:

- ¼ cup almond milk
- ¼ cup coconut sugar
- ¼ tsp. cinnamon
- ½ tsp. salt
- 1 cup white all-purpose flour
- 1 Tbsp. coconut oil, melted
- 1 tsp. baking powder
- 2 Tbsps. aquafaba or liquid from canned chickpeas

Directions:

1. In a mixing bowl, mix the flour, sugar, and baking powder. Add the salt and cinnamon and mix well.
2. In another bowl, mix together the coconut oil, aquafaba, and almond milk.
3. Gently pour the dry ingredients to the wet ingredients. Mix together until well combined or until you form a sticky dough.
4. Place the dough in the refrigerator to rest for at least an hour.
5. Preheat the air fryer to 370°F.
6. Create small balls of the dough and place inside the air fryer and cook for 10 minutes. Do not shake the air fryer.
7. Once cooked, sprinkle with sugar and cinnamon.
8. Serve with your breakfast coffee.

Nutrition:

Calories: 120
Carbohydrates: 21.62g
Protein: 2.31g
Fat: 2.76g

253. Oriental Coconut Cake

Preparation Time: 10 minutes
Cooking Time: 40 minutes
Servings: 6

Ingredients:

- 1 cup gluten-free flour
- 2 eggs
- 1/2 cup flaked coconut
- 1-1/2 tsps. baking powder
- 1/2 tsp. baking soda
- 1/2 tsp. xanthan gum
- 1/2 tsp. salt
- 1/2 cup coconut milk
- 1/2 cup vegetable oil
- 1/2 tsp. vanilla extract
- 1/4 cup chopped walnuts
- 3/4 cup Splenda

Directions:

1. In blender blend all wet ingredients. In a bowl add the dry ingredients and blend thoroughly with the wet ingredients.
2. Lightly grease baking pan of the air fryer with cooking spray.
3. Pour in batter. Cover pan with foil.
4. Bake at 330°F for 30 minutes.
5. Let it rest for 10 minutes.
6. Serve and enjoy.

Nutrition:

Calories: 359
Carbs: 35.2g
Protein: 4.3g
Fat: 22.3g

254. Coffee 'n Blueberry Cake

Preparation Time: 10 minutes
Cooking Time: 35 minutes
Servings: 6

Ingredients:

- 1 cup all-purpose sugar substitute blend
- 1 egg
- ½ cup butter, softened
- ½ cup fresh or frozen blueberries
- ½ cup sour cream
- ½ tsp. baking powder
- ½ tsp. ground cinnamon
- ½ tsp. vanilla extract
- ¼ cup brown sugar substitute
- ¼ cup chopped pecans
- 1/8 tsp. salt
- 1 ½ tsps. confectioners' sugar for dusting (optional)
- ¾ cup plus 1 Tbsp. all-purpose flour

Directions:

1. In a small bowl, mix pecans, cinnamon, and brown sugar.
2. In a blender, blend all wet ingredients. Add dry ngredients except for confectioner's sugar and blueberries in a bowl. Add the wet ingredients and mix well until smooth and creamy.
3. Lightly grease the baking pan of the air fryer with cooking spray.
4. Pour half of batter in pan. Sprinkle half of pecan mixture and blueberries on top. Pour the remaining batter. And then top with remaining pecan mixture.
5. Cover pan with foil.
6. Bake for 35 minutes on 300°F.
7. Serve and enjoy with a dusting of confectioner's sugar.

Nutrition:

Calories: 471
Carbs: 59.5g
Protein: 4.1g
Fat: 24.0g

255. Mouth-Watering Strawberry Cobbler

Preparation Time: 10 minutes
Cooking Time: 25 minutes
Servings: 4

Ingredients:

- 1 Tbsp. butter, diced
- 1 Tbsp. and 2 tsps. butter
- 1 ½ tsps. cornstarch
- ½ cup water
- 1 ½ cups strawberries, hulled
- ½ cup all-purpose flour
- 1 ½ tsps. Swerve
- ¼ cup Swerve
- ¼ tsp. salt
- ¼ cup heavy whipping cream
- ¾ tsp. baking powder

Directions:

1. Lightly grease baking pan of air fryer with cooking spray. Add water, cornstarch, and ¼ cup Swerve. Cook for 10 minutes at 390°F or until hot and thick. Add strawberries and mix well. Dot tops with 1 Tbsp. butter.
2. In a bowl, mix salt, baking powder, remaining sugar, and flour. Cut in 1 Tbsp. and 2 tsp. butter. Mix in cream. Spoon on top of berries.
3. Cook for 15 minutes at 390°F, until tops are lightly browned.
4. Serve and enjoy.

Nutrition:

Calories: 255
Carbs: 32.0g
Protein: 2.4g
Fat: 13.0g

256. Walnut Carrot Cake

Preparation Time: 10 minutes
Cooking Time: 40 minutes
Servings: 8

Ingredients:

- 3 eggs
- 1 tsp. baking powder
- 2/3 cup swerve
- 1 cup almond flour
- ¾ cup walnuts, chopped
- 1 cup carrot, grated
- ½ cup heavy cream
- ¼ cup coconut oil
- 1 tsp. apple pie spice

Directions:

1. Preheat the air fryer to 300°F.
2. Grease a baking dish with cooking spray and set it aside.
3. Add all ingredients into a large bowl and mix until well combined.
4. Pour batter into the baking dish and cover the dish with foil.
5. Bake for 35 minutes on 300°F.
6. Slice and serve.

Nutrition:

Calories: 208
Fat: 19.9 g
Carbohydrates: 24.1 g
Sugar: 21.1 g
Protein: 5.9 g
Cholesterol: 72 mg

Chapter 9. Vegetarian Recipes

N. 259 Fried Green Beans with Pecorino Romano
N. 262 Rainbow Vegetable Fritters
N. 274 Family Vegetable Gratin
N. 283 Roasted Broccoli with Sesame Seeds
N. 296 Onion Pasties
N. 300 Carrot and Oat Balls

257. Fried Peppers with Sriracha Mayo

Preparation Time: 20 minutes
Cooking Time: 10 minutes
Servings: 2

Ingredients:

- 4 bell peppers, seeded and sliced (1-inch pieces
- 1 onion, sliced (1-inch pieces)
- 1 Tbsp. olive oil
- ½ tsp. dried rosemary
- ½ tsp. dried basil
- Kosher salt, to taste
- ¼ tsp. ground black pepper
- 1/3 cup mayonnaise
- 1/3 tsp. Sriracha

Directions:

1. Sprinkle the bell peppers and onions with olive oil, rosemary, basil, salt, and black pepper.
2. Place the peppers and onions on an even layer in the cooking basket. Cook at 400°F for 12 to 14 minutes.
3. Meanwhile, make the sauce by whisking the mayonnaise and Sriracha. Serve immediately.

Nutrition:
Calories: 346
Fat: 34.1 g
Carbs: 9.5 g
Protein: 2.3 g
Sugars: 4.9 g

258. Classic Fried Pickles

Preparation Time: 20 minutes
Cooking Time: 10 minutes
Servings: 2

Ingredients:

- 1 egg, whisked
- 2 Tbsps. buttermilk
- ½ cup fresh breadcrumbs
- ¼ cup Romano cheese, grated
- ½ tsp. onion powder
- ½ tsp. garlic powder
- 1 ½ cups dill pickle chips, pressed dry with kitchen towels

Mayo Sauce:

- ¼ cup mayonnaise
- ½ Tbsp. mustard
- ½ tsp. molasses
- 1 Tbsp. sugar-free ketchup
- ¼ tsp. ground black pepper

Directions:

1. In a small bowl, whisk the egg with the buttermilk.
2. In another bowl, mix the breadcrumbs, cheese, onion powder, and garlic powder.
3. Dip the pickle chips in the egg mixture, then dredge it in the breadcrumb/cheese mixture.
4. Cook in the preheated air fryer at 400°F for 5 minutes; shake the basket and cook for 5 minutes more.
5. Meanwhile, mix all the sauce ingredients until well combined. Serve the fried pickles with the mayo sauce for dipping.

Nutrition:
Calories: 342
Fat: 28.5 g
Carbs: 12.5 g
Protein: 9.1 g
Sugars: 4.9 g

259. Fried Green Beans with Pecorino Romano

Preparation Time: 15 minutes
Cooking Time: 10 minutes
Servings: 3

Ingredients:

- 2 Tbsps. buttermilk
- 1 egg
- 4 Tbsps. cornmeal
- 4 Tbsps. tortilla chips, crushed
- 4 Tbsps. Pecorino Romano cheese, finely grated
- Coarse salt and crushed black pepper, to taste
- 1 tsp. smoked paprika
- 12 oz. green beans, trimmed

Directions:

1. In a small bowl, whisk together the buttermilk and egg.
2. In a separate bowl, combine the cornmeal, tortilla chips, Pecorino Romano cheese, salt, black pepper, and paprika.
3. Dip the green beans in the egg mixture, then dredge it in the cornmeal/cheese mixture. Place the green beans in the lightly greased cooking basket.
4. Cook in the preheated air fryer at 390°F for 4 minutes. Shake the basket and cook for a further 3 minutes.
5. Taste, adjust the seasonings, and serve with a dipping sauce if desired. Bon appétit!

Nutrition:
Calories: 340
Fat: 9.7 g
Carbs: 50.9 g
Protein: 12.8 g
Sugars: 4.7 g

260. Spicy Glazed Carrots

Preparation Time: 20 minutes
Cooking Time: 10 minutes
Servings: 3

Ingredients:

- 1 lb. carrots, cut into matchsticks
- 2 Tbsps. peanut oil
- 1 Tbsp. agave syrup
- 1 jalapeño, seeded and minced
- ¼ tsp. dill
- ½ tsp. basil
- Salt and white pepper, to taste

Directions:

1. Pre-heat your air fryer to 380°F.
2. Toss all ingredients together and place them in the air fryer basket.
3. Cook for 15 minutes, shaking the basket halfway through the cooking time. Transfer to a serving platter and enjoy!

Nutrition:
Calories: 162
Fat: 9.3 g
Carbs: 20.1 g
Protein: 1.4 g
Sugars: 12.8 g

261. Corn on the Cob with Herb Butter

Preparation Time: 15 minutes
Cooking Time: 10 minutes
Servings: 2

Ingredients:

- 2 ears new corn, shucked and cut into halves
- 2 Tbsps. butter, room temperature
- 1 tsp. granulated garlic
- ½ tsp. fresh ginger, grated
- Sea salt and pepper, to taste
- 1 Tbsp. fresh rosemary, chopped
- 1 Tbsp. fresh basil, chopped
- 2 Tbsps. fresh chives, roughly chopped

Directions:

1. Cover the corn with cooking spray. Cook at 395°F for 6 minutes, turning them over halfway through the cooking time.
2. For the time being, mix the butter with the granulated garlic, ginger, salt, black pepper, rosemary, and basil.
3. Spread the butter mixture all over the corn on the cob. Cook in the preheated air fryer for an additional 2 minutes. Bon appétit!

Nutrition:
Calories: 239
Fat: 13.3 g
Carbs: 30.2 g
Protein: 5.4 g
Sugars: 5.8 g

262. Rainbow Vegetable Fritters

Preparation Time: 20 minutes
Cooking Time: 10 minutes
Servings: 2

Ingredients:

- 1 zucchini, grated and squeezed
- 1 cup corn kernels
- ½ cup canned green peas
- 4 Tbsps. all-purpose flour
- 2 Tbsp. fresh shallots, minced
- 1 tsp. fresh garlic, minced
- 1 Tbsp. peanut oil
- Sea salt and pepper, to taste
- 1 tsp. cayenne pepper

Directions:

1. In a mixing bowl, thoroughly combine all ingredients until everything is well incorporated.
2. Shape the mixture into patties. Cover the air fryer basket with cooking spray.
3. Cook in the preheated air fryer at 365°F for 6 minutes. Flip them over and cook for a further 6 minutes
4. Serve immediately and enjoy!

Nutrition:
Calories: 215
Fat: 8.4 g
Carbs: 31.6 g
Protein: 6 g
Sugars: 4.1 g

263. Mediterranean Vegetable Skewers

Preparation Time: 30 minutes
Cooking Time: 10 minutes
Servings: 4

Ingredients:

- 2 medium-sized zucchinis, cut into 1-inch pieces
- 2 red bell peppers, cut into 1-inch pieces
- 1 green bell pepper, cut into 1-inch pieces
- 1 red onion, cut into 1-inch pieces
- 2 Tbsps. olive oil
- Sea salt, to taste
- ½ tsp. black pepper, preferably freshly cracked
- ½ tsp. red pepper flakes

Directions:

1. Soak the wooden skewers in water for 15 minutes.
2. Thread the vegetables on skewers, drizzle olive oil all over the vegetable skewers, sprinkle with spices.
3. Cook in the preheated air fryer at 400°F for 13 minutes. Serve warm and enjoy!

Nutrition:
Calories: 138
Fat: 10.2 g
Carbs: 10.2 g
Protein: 2.2 g
Sugars: 6.6 g

264. Roasted Veggies with Yogurt-Tahini Sauce

Preparation Time: 20 minutes
Cooking Time: 10 minutes
Servings: 4

Ingredients:

- 1 lb. Brussels sprouts
- 1 lb. button mushrooms
- 2 Tbsps. olive oil
- ½ tsp. white pepper
- ½ tsp. dried dill weed
- ½ tsp. cayenne pepper
- ½ tsp. celery seeds
- ½ tsp. mustard seeds
- Salt, to taste

Yogurt Tahini Sauce:

- 1 cup plain yogurt
- 2 heaping Tbsp. tahini paste
- 1 Tbsp. lemon juice
- 1 Tbsp. extra-virgin olive oil
- ½ tsp. Aleppo pepper, minced

Directions:

1. Toss the Brussels sprouts and mushrooms with olive oil and spices. Preheat your air fryer to 380°F.
2. Add the Brussels sprouts to the cooking basket and cook for 10 minutes.
3. Add the mushrooms, turn the temperature to 390°F and cook for 6 minutes more.
4. While the vegetables are cooking, make the sauce by whisking all the sauce ingredients. Serve the warm vegetables with the sauce on the side. Bon appétit!

Nutrition:
Calories: 254
Fat: 17.2 g
Carbs: 19.6 g
Protein: 11.1 g
Sugars: 8.1 g

265. Swiss Cheese and Vegetable Casserole

Preparation Time: 50 minutes
Cooking Time: 10 minutes
Servings: 4

Ingredients:

- 1 lb. potatoes, peeled and sliced (1/4-inch thick)
- 2 Tbsps. olive oil
- ½ tsp. red pepper flakes, crushed
- ½ tsp. freshly ground black pepper
- Salt, to taste
- 3 bell peppers, thinly sliced
- 1 serrano pepper, thinly sliced
- 2 medium-sized tomatoes, sliced
- 1 leek, thinly sliced
- 2 garlic cloves, minced
- 1 cup Swiss cheese, shredded

Directions:

1. Start by warming your air fryer to 350°F. Grease a casserole dish with cooking oil.
2. Place the potatoes in the casserole dish in an even layer; drizzle 1 Tbsp. of olive oil over the top, then sprinkle with the red pepper, black pepper, and salt.
3. Add 2 bell peppers and 1/2 of the leeks. Add the tomatoes and the remaining 1 Tbsp. of olive oil.
4. Add the remaining peppers, leeks, and minced garlic. Top with the cheese.
5. Cover the casserole with foil and bake for 32 minutes. Remove the foil and increase the temperature to 400°F; bake an additional 16 minutes. Bon appétit!

Nutrition:
Calories: 328
Fat: 16.5 g
Carbs: 33.1 g
Protein: 13.1 g
Sugars: 7.6 g

266. American-Style Brussels Sprout Salad

Preparation Time: 35 minutes
Cooking Time: 10 minutes
Servings: 4

Ingredients:

- 1 lb. Brussels sprouts
- 1 apple, cored and diced
- ½ cup mozzarella cheese, crumbled
- ½ cup pomegranate seeds
- 1 small-sized red onion, chopped
- 4 eggs, hardboiled and sliced

Dressing:

- ¼ cup olive oil

- 2 Tbsps. champagne vinegar
- 1 tsp. Dijon mustard
- 1 tsp. honey
- Sea salt and ground black pepper, to taste

Directions:

1. Start by preheating your air fryer to 380°F.
2. Add the Brussels sprouts to the cooking basket. Spray with cooking spray and cook for 15 minutes. Let it cool to room temperature for about 15 minutes.
3. Toss the Brussels sprouts with the apple, cheese, pomegranate seeds, and red onion.
4. Mix all ingredients for the dressing, add it to the vegetables and toss to combine well. Serve topped with hard-boiled eggs. Bon appétit!

Nutrition:
Calories: 319
Fat: 18.5 g
Carbs: 27 g
Protein: 14.7 g
Sugars: 14.6 g

267. The Best Cauliflower Tater Tots

Preparation Time: 25 minutes
Cooking Time: 10 minutes
Servings: 4

Ingredients:

- 1 lb. cauliflower florets
- 2 eggs
- 1 Tbsp. olive oil
- 2 Tbsps. scallions, chopped
- 1 garlic clove, minced
- 1 cup Colby cheese, shredded
- ½ cup breadcrumbs
- Sea salt and ground black pepper, to taste
- ¼ tsp. dried dill weed
- 1 tsp. paprika

Directions:

1. Blanch the cauliflower in salted boiling water for about 3 to 4 minutes until al dente. Drain well and pulse in a food processor.
2. Add it to the remaining ingredients; mix to combine well. Shape the cauliflower mixture into bite-sized tots.
3. Spray the air fryer basket with cooking spray.
4. Cook in the preheated air fryer at 375°F for 16 minutes, shaking halfway through the cooking time. Serve with your favorite sauce for dipping. Bon appétit!

Nutrition:
Calories: 267
Fat: 19.2 g
Carbs: 9.6 g
Protein: 14.9 g
Sugars: 2.9 g

268. Three-Cheese Stuffed Mushrooms

Preparation Time: 15 minutes
Cooking Time: 10 minutes
Servings: 3

Ingredients:

- 9 large button mushrooms, stems removed
- 1 Tbsp. olive oil
- Salt and ground black pepper, to taste
- ½ tsp. dried rosemary
- 6 Tbsps. Swiss cheese shredded
- 6 Tbsps. Romano cheese, shredded
- 6 Tbsps. cream cheese
- 1 tsp. soy sauce
- 1 tsp. garlic, minced
- 3 Tbsps. green onion, minced

Directions:

1. Brush the mushroom caps with olive oil; sprinkle with salt, pepper, and rosemary.
2. In a mixing bowl, thoroughly combine the remaining ingredients, mix them well, and divide the filling mixture among the mushroom caps.
3. Cook in the preheated air fryer at 390°F for 7 minutes.
4. Let the mushrooms cool slightly before serving. Bon appétit!

Nutrition:
Calories: 345
Fat: 28 g
Carbs: 11.2 g
Protein: 14.4 g
Sugars: 8.1 g

269. Sweet Corn Fritters with Avocado

Preparation Time: 20 minutes
Cooking Time: 10 minutes
Servings: 3

Ingredients:

- 2 cups sweet corn kernels
- 1 small-sized onion, chopped
- 1 garlic clove, minced
- 2 eggs, whisked
- 1 tsp. baking powder
- 2 Tbsps. fresh cilantro, chopped
- Sea salt and ground black pepper, to taste
- 1 avocado, peeled, pitted, and diced
- 2 Tbsp. sweet chili sauce

Directions:

1. In a mixing bowl, thoroughly combine the corn, onion, garlic, eggs, baking powder, cilantro, salt, and black pepper.
2. Shape the corn mixture into 6 patties and transfer them to the lightly greased air fryer basket.
3. Cook in the preheated air fry at 370°F for 8 minutes; turn them over and cook for 7 minutes longer.
4. Serve the patties with avocado and chili sauce.

Nutrition:
Calories: 383
Fat: 21.3 g
Carbs: 42.8 g
Protein: 12.7 g
Sugars: 9.2 g

270. Greek-Style Vegetable Bake

Preparation Time: 35 minutes
Cooking Time: 10 minutes
Servings: 4

Ingredients:

- 1 eggplant, peeled and sliced
- 2 bell peppers, seeded and sliced
- 1 red onion, sliced
- 1 tsp. fresh garlic, minced
- 4 Tbsps. olive oil
- 1 tsp. mustard
- 1 tsp. dried oregano
- 1 tsp. smoked paprika
- Salt and ground black pepper, to taste
- 1 tomato, sliced
- 6 oz. halloumi cheese, sliced lengthwise

Directions:

1. Start by preheating your air fryer to 370°F. Spray a baking pan with nonstick cooking spray.
2. Place the eggplant, peppers, onion, and garlic on the baking pan's bottom. Add the olive oil, mustard, and spices. Transfer to the air fryer and cook for 14 minutes.
3. Top with the tomatoes and cheese; increase the temperature to 390°F and cook for 5 minutes more until bubbling. Let it sit on a cooling rack for 10 minutes before serving.
4. Bon appétit!

Nutrition:
Calories: 296
Fat: 22.9 g
Carbs: 16.1 g
Protein: 9.3 g
Sugars: 9.9 g

271. Japanese Tempura Bowl

Preparation Time: 20 minutes
Cooking Time: 10 minutes
Servings: 3

Ingredients:

- 1 cup all-purpose flour
- Kosher salt and ground black pepper, to taste
- ½ tsp. paprika
- 2 eggs
- 3 Tbsps. soda water
- 1 cup panko crumbs
- 2 Tbsps. olive oil
- 1 cup green beans
- 1 onion, cut into rings
- 1 zucchini, cut into slices
- 2 Tbsps. soy sauce
- 1 Tbsp. mirin
- 1 tsp. dashi granules

Directions:

1. In a small bowl, mix the flour, salt, black pepper, and paprika. In a separate bowl, whisk the eggs and soda water. In a third shallow bowl, combine the panko crumbs with olive oil.
2. Dip the vegetables in the flour mixture, then in the egg mixture; lastly, roll over the panko mixture to coat evenly.
3. Cook in the preheated air fryer at 400°F for 10 minutes, shaking the basket halfway through the cooking time. Work in batches until the vegetables are crispy and golden brown.
4. Then, make the sauce by whisking the soy sauce, mirin and dashi granules. Bon appétit!

Nutrition:
Calories: 446
Fat: 14.7 g
Carbs: 63.5 g
Protein: 14.6 g
Sugars: 3.8 g

272. Balsamic Root Vegetables

Preparation Time: 25 minutes
Cooking Time: 10 minutes
Servings: 3

Ingredients:

- 2 potatoes, cut into 1 ½ -inch pieces
- 2 carrots, cut into 1 ½ -inch pieces
- 2 parsnips, cut into 1 ½ -inch pieces
- 1 onion, cut into 1 ½-inch pieces
- Pink Himalayan salt and ground black pepper, to taste
- ¼ tsp. smoked paprika

- 1 tsp. garlic powder
- ½ tsp. dried thyme
- ½ tsp. dried marjoram
- 2 Tbsps. olive oil
- 2 Tbsps. balsamic vinegar

Directions:

1. Toss all ingredients in a large mixing bowl.
2. Roast in the preheated air fryer at 400°F for 10 minutes. Shake the basket and cook for 7 minutes more.
3. Serve with some extra fresh herbs if desired. Bon appétit!

Nutrition:
Calories: 405
Fat: 9.7 g
Carbs: 74.7 g
Protein: 7.7 g
Sugars: 15.2 g

273. Winter Vegetable Braise

Preparation Time: 25 minutes
Cooking Time: 10 minutes
Servings: 2

Ingredients:

- 4 potatoes, peeled and cut into 1-inch pieces
- 1 celery root, peeled and cut into 1-inch pieces
- 1 cup winter squash
- 2 Tbsps. unsalted butter, melted
- ½ cup chicken broth
- ¼ cup tomato sauce
- 1 tsp. parsley
- 1 tsp. rosemary
- 1 tsp. thyme

Directions:

1. Start by preheating your air fryer to 370°F. Add all ingredients to a lightly greased casserole dish. Stir to combine well.
2. Bake in the preheated air fryer for 10 minutes. Gently stir the vegetables with a large spoon and increase the temperature to 400°F; cook for 10 minutes more.
3. Serve in individual bowls with a few drizzles of lemon juice. Bon appétit!

Nutrition:
Calories: 358
Fat: 12.3 g
Carbs: 55.7 g
Protein: 7.7 g
Sugars: 7.4 g

274. Family Vegetable Gratin

Preparation Time: 35 minutes
Cooking Time: 10 minutes
Servings: 4

Ingredients:

- 1 lb. Chinese cabbage, roughly chopped
- 2 bell peppers, seeded and sliced
- 1 jalapeno pepper, seeded and sliced
- 1 onion, thickly sliced
- 2 garlic cloves, sliced
- 1/2 stick butter
- 4 Tbsps. all-purpose flour
- 1 cup milk
- 1 cup cream cheese
- Sea salt and freshly ground black pepper, to taste
- 1/2 tsp. cayenne pepper
- 1 cup Monterey Jack cheese, shredded

Directions:

1. Heat a pan with salted water and bring to a boil. Boil the Chinese cabbage for 2 to 3 minutes. Transfer the Chinese cabbage to cold water to stop the cooking process.
2. Place the Chinese cabbage in a lightly greased casserole dish. Add the peppers, onion, and garlic.
3. Next, melt the butter in a saucepan over moderate heat. Gradually add the flour and cook for 2 minutes to form a paste.
4. Slowly pour in the milk, stirring continuously until a thick sauce forms. Add the cream cheese.
5. Season with salt, black pepper, and cayenne pepper. Add the mixture to the casserole dish.
6. Top with the shredded Monterey Jack cheese and bake in the preheated air fryer at 390°F for 25 minutes. Serve hot.

Nutrition:
Calories: 373
Fat: 26.1 g
Carbs: 17.7 g
Protein: 18.7 g
Sugars. 7.7 g

275. Sweet-and-Sour Mixed Veggies

Preparation Time: 25 minutes
Cooking Time: 10 minutes
Servings: 4

Ingredients:

- ½ lb. sterling asparagus, cut into 1 ½-inch pieces
- ½ lb. broccoli, cut into 1 ½-inch pieces
- ½ lb. carrots, cut into 1 ½-inch pieces
- 2 Tbsps. peanut oil
- Salt and white pepper, to taste

- ½ cup water
- 4 Tbsps. raisins
- 2 Tbsps. honey
- 2 Tbsps. apple cider vinegar

Directions:

1. Place the vegetables in a single layer in the lightly greased cooking basket. Drizzle the peanut oil over the vegetables.
2. Sprinkle with salt and white pepper.
3. Cook at 380°F for 15 minutes, shaking the basket halfway through the cooking time.
4. Add 1/2 cup of water to a saucepan; bring to a rapid boil and add the raisins, honey, and vinegar. Simmer for 5 to 7 minutes or until the sauce has been reduced by half.
5. Spoon the sauce over the warm vegetables and serve immediately. Bon appétit!

Nutrition:
Calories: 153
Fat: 7.1 g
Carbs: 21.6 g
Protein: 3.6 g
Sugars: 14.2 g

276. Green Onions & Parmesan Tomatoes

Preparation Time: 5 minutes
Cooking Time: 15 minutes
Servings: 4
Ingredients:

- 1 Tbsp. olive oil
- 1/2 cup Parmesan, grated
- 1/2 tsp. thyme, dried
- 2 garlic cloves, minced
- 2 green onions, chopped
- 4 large tomatoes, cut into slices
- Salt and pepper to season

Directions:

1. Heat the air fryer to 390°F.
2. Season tomato slices with garlic, olive oil, thyme, salt, and pepper. Top with chopped green onions and Parmesan cheese.
3. Place tomatoes in the air fryer basket and cook for about 15 minutes.
4. Serve.

Nutrition:
Calories: 68
Fat: 3.8 g
Carbohydrates: 68 g
Protein: 1.9 g

277. Zucchini Fritters

Preparation Time: 20 minutes
Cooking Time: 12 minutes
Servings: 4
Ingredients:

- 1 egg
- 1 Tbsp. salt
- 1 tsp. garlic powder
- 1/4 tsp. ground black pepper
- 1/4 tsp. onion powder
- 1/4 tsp. paprika
- 2 medium zucchinis, ends trimmed
- 3 Tbsps. almond flour

Directions:

1. Wash and pat dry the zucchini, then cut off ends and grate the zucchini.
2. Place grated zucchini in a colander, sprinkle with salt and let it rest for 10 minutes.
3. Wrap zucchini in a kitchen cloth and squeeze moisture from it as much as possible and place dried zucchini in another bowl.
4. Add remaining ingredients into the zucchini and then stir until mixed.
5. Take air fryer basket, line it with parchment paper, and grease it with oil and drop zucchini mixture on it by the spoonful, about 1-inch apart and then spray well with oil.
6. Switch on the air fryer, insert fryer basket, then shut the lid, set the fryer at 360°F and cook the fritter for 12 minutes until nicely golden and cooked, flipping the fritters halfway through the frying.
7. Serve straight away.

Nutrition:
Calories: 57
Carbs: 8 g
Fat: 1 g
Protein: 3 g
Fiber: 1 g

278. Air Fryer Asparagus

Preparation Time: 15 minutes
Cooking Time: 7 minutes
Servings: 4
Ingredients:

- 1 lb. asparagus, trimmed
- 2 tsp. extra-virgin olive oil
- ¼ tsp. ground pepper
- 1/8 tsp. salt

Directions:

1. Preheat the air fryer to 400°F.

2. In a bowl, season the asparagus with pepper, oil and salt. Arrange the asparagus in a single layer in the air fryer's basket.
3. Cook for 7 minutes or until they are tender.
4. Serve immediately.

Nutrition:
Calories: 43
Fat: 2 g
Protein: 3 g
Carbohydrates: 4 g
Fiber: 3 g

279. Bacon Avocado Fries

Preparation Time: 20 minutes
Cooking Time: 8 minutes
Servings: 1

Ingredients:

- 2 medium, ripe avocados, pitted and peeled
- 12 bacon strips

Sauce:

- 1 tsp. grated lime zest
- 1/2 cup mayonnaise
- 2 Tbsps. lime juice
- 2 Tbsps. Sriracha chili sauce

Directions:

1. Preheat the air fryer to 400°F.
2. Cut avocado in 6 parts.
3. Wrap each avocado wedge with 1 slice of bacon.
4. Arrange the wedges on the air fryer's basket and cook for about 12 minutes.
5. Combine the mayonnaise, lime juice, Sriracha sauce and zest in a small bowl.
6. Enjoy the avocado wedges with the sauce.

Nutrition:
Calories: 142
Fat: 9 g
Protein: 3.3 g
Carbohydrates: 2.9 g
Fiber: 2.2 g

280. Glazed Veggies

Preparation Time: 20 minutes
Cooking Time: 20 minutes
Servings: 4

Ingredients:

- 2 ounces cherry tomatoes
- 1 large parsnip, peeled and chopped
- 1 large carrot, peeled and chopped
- 1 large zucchini, chopped
- 1 green bell pepper, seeded and chopped
- 6 Tbsps. olive oil, divided
- 3 Tbsps. honey
- 1 tsp. Dijon mustard
- 1 tsp. mixed dried herbs
- 1 tsp. garlic paste
- Salt and black pepper, to taste

Directions:

1. Preheat the Air fryer to 350°F and grease an air fryer pan.
2. Arrange cherry tomatoes, parsnip, carrot, zucchini and bell pepper in the air fryer pan and drizzle with 3 tablespoons of olive oil.
3. Cook for about 15 minutes and remove from the air fryer.
4. Mix remaining olive oil, honey, mustard, herbs, garlic, salt, and black pepper in a bowl.
5. Pour this mixture over the vegetables in the air fryer pan and set the air fryer to 390°F.
6. Cook for about 5 minutes and serve hot.

Nutrition:
Calories: 288
Fat: 21.4g
Carbohydrates: 26.7g
Sugar: 18.7g
Protein: 2.1g
Sodium: 79mg

281. Sweet and Spicy Parsnips

Preparation Time: 15 minutes
Cooking Time: 44 minutes
Servings: 6

Ingredients:

- 2 lbs. parsnip, peeled and cut into 1-inch chunks
- 1 Tbsp. butter, melted
- 2 Tbsps. honey
- 1 Tbsp. dried parsley flakes, crushed
- ¼ tsp. red pepper flakes, crushed
- Salt and ground black pepper, to taste

Directions:

1. Preheat the air fryer to 355°F and grease an air fryer basket.
2. Mix the parsnips and butter in a bowl and toss to coat well.
3. Arrange the parsnip chunks in the air fryer basket and cook for about 40 minutes.
4. Mix the remaining ingredients in another large bowl and stir in the cooked parsnip chunks.
5. Transfer the parsnip mixture in the air fryer basket and cook for about 4 minutes.
6. Dish out the parsnip chunks onto serving plates and serve hot.

Nutrition:
Calories: 155
Fat: 2.4 g
Carbohydrates: 33.1g
Sugar: 13g
Protein: 1.9g
Sodium: 57mg

282. Easy Sweet Potato Bake

Preparation Time: 35 minutes
Cooking Time: 30 minutes
Servings: 3
Ingredients:

- 1 stick butter, melted
- 1 lb. sweet potatoes, mashed
- 2 eggs, beaten
- 1/3 cup coconut milk
- ¼ cup flour
- ½ cup fresh breadcrumbs

Directions:

1. Start by preheating your air fryer to 325°F.
2. Spray a casserole dish with cooking oil.
3. In a mixing bowl, combine all ingredients, except for the breadcrumbs and 1 tablespoon butter. Spoon the mixture into the prepared casserole dish.
4. Top with the breadcrumbs and brush the top with the remaining 1 tablespoon butter. Bake in the preheated air fryer for 30 minutes. Bon appétit!

Nutrition:
Calories: 409
Fat: 26.1 g
Carbohydrates: 38.3 g
Protein: 7.2 g

283. Roasted Broccoli with Sesame Seeds

Preparation Time: 15 minutes
Cooking Time: 10 minutes
Servings: 2
Ingredients:

- 1 lb. broccoli florets
- 2 Tbsps. sesame oil
- ½ tsp. shallot powder
- ½ tsp. porcini powder
- 1 tsp. garlic powder
- Sea salt and black pepper, ground, to season
- ½ tsp. cumin powder
- ¼ tsp. paprika
- 2 Tbsps. sesame seeds

Directions:

1. Preheat the air fryer to 400°F.
2. Blanch broccoli in boiling salted water for about 4 minutes.
3. After draining them well, grease them lightly and transfer them to the air fryer basket.
4. Add the oil, porcini powder, black pepper, shallot powder, garlic powder, salt, cumin powder, paprika, and sesame seeds.
5. Cook for about 6 minutes, turning halfway through cooking.

Nutrition:
Calories: 267
Fat: 12.5 g
Carbohydrates: 20.2 g
Protein: 8.9 g

284. Herbed Carrots

Preparation Time: 15 minutes
Cooking Time: 14 minutes
Servings: 8
Ingredients:

- 6 large carrots, peeled and sliced lengthwise
- 2 Tbsps. olive oil
- ½ Tbsp. fresh oregano, chopped
- ½ Tbsp. fresh parsley, chopped
- Salt and black pepper, to taste
- 2 Tbsps. olive oil, divided
- ½ cup fat-free Italian dressing
- Salt, to taste

Directions:

1. Preheat the air fryer to 360°F and grease an air fryer basket.
2. Mix the carrot slices and olive oil in a bowl and toss to coat well.
3. Arrange the carrot slices in the air fryer basket and cook for about 12 minutes.
4. Sprinkle the carrots with herbs, salt and black pepper.
5. Cook for 2 more minutes.
6. Dish out and serve hot with salad dressing.

Nutrition:
Calories: 93
Fat: 7.2g
Carbohydrates: 7.3g
Sugar: 3.8g
Protein: 0.7g
Sodium: 252mg

285. Curried Eggplant

Preparation Time: 15 minutes
Cooking Time: 10 minutes
Servings: 2
Ingredients:

- 1 large eggplant, cut into ½-inch thick slices
- 1 garlic clove, minced
- ½ fresh red chili, chopped
- 1 Tbsp. vegetable oil
- ¼ tsp. curry powder
- Salt, to taste

Directions:

1. Preheat the air fryer to 300°F and grease an air fryer basket.

2. Mix all the ingredients in a bowl and toss to coat well.
3. Arrange the eggplant slices in the air fryer basket and cook for about 10 minutes, tossing once in between.
4. Dish out onto serving plates and serve hot.

Nutrition:
Calories: 121
Fat: 7.3g
Carbohydrates: 14.2g
Sugar: 7g
Protein: 2.4g
Sodium: 83mg

286. Herbed Eggplant

Preparation Time: 15 minutes
Cooking Time: 15 minutes
Servings: 2

Ingredients:

- 1 large eggplant, cubed
- ½ tsp. dried marjoram, crushed
- ½ tsp. dried oregano, crushed
- ½ tsp. dried thyme, crushed
- ½ tsp. garlic powder
- Salt and black pepper, to taste
- Olive oil cooking spray

Directions:

1. Preheat the air fryer to 390°F and grease an air fryer basket.
2. Mix herbs, garlic powder, salt, and black pepper in a bowl.
3. Spray the eggplant cubes with cooking spray and rub with the herb mixture.
4. Arrange the eggplant cubes in the air fryer basket and cook for about 15 minutes, flipping twice in between.
5. Dish out onto serving plates and serve hot.

Nutrition:
Calories: 62
Fat: 0.5g
Carbohydrates: 14.5g
Sugar: 7.1g
Protein: 2.4g
Sodium: 83mg

287. Salsa Stuffed Eggplants

Preparation Time: 15 minutes
Cooking Time: 25 minutes
Servings: 2

Ingredients:

- 1 large eggplant
- 8 cherry tomatoes, quartered
- ½ Tbsp. fresh parsley
- 2 tsps. olive oil, divided
- 2 tsps. fresh lemon juice, divided
- 2 Tbsps. tomato salsa
- Salt and black pepper, as required

Directions:

1. Preheat the air fryer to 390°F and grease an air fryer basket.
2. Arrange the eggplant into the air fryer basket and cook for about 15 minutes.
3. Cut the eggplant in half lengthwise and drizzle evenly with one teaspoon of oil.
4. Set the air fryer to 355°F and arrange the eggplant into the Air fryer basket, cut-side up.
5. Cook for another 10 minutes and dish out into a plate.
6. Scoop out the flesh from the eggplant and transfer into a bowl.
7. Mix the tomatoes, salsa, parsley, salt, black pepper, remaining oil, and lemon juice.
8. Squeeze lemon juice on the eggplant halves and stuff with the salsa mixture to serve.

Nutrition:
Calories: 192
Fat: 6.1g
Carbohydrates: 33.8g
Sugar: 20.4g
Protein: 6.9g
Sodium: 204mg

288. Sesame Seeds Bok Choy

Preparation Time: 10 minutes
Cooking Time: 6 minutes
Servings: 4

Ingredients:

- 4 bunches baby bok choy, bottoms removed and leaves separated
- 1 tsp. sesame seeds
- Olive oil cooking spray
- 1 tsp. garlic powder

Directions:

1. Preheat the air fryer to 325°F and grease an air fryer basket.
2. Arrange the bok choy leaves into the air fryer basket and spray with the cooking spray.
3. Sprinkle with garlic powder and cook for about 6 minutes, shaking twice in between.
4. Dish out in the bok choy onto serving plates and serve garnished with sesame seeds.

Nutrition:
Calories: 26
Fat: 0.7g
Carbohydrates: 4g
Sugar: 1.9g
Protein: 2.5g
Sodium: 98mg

289. Basil Tomatoes

Preparation Time: 10 minutes
Cooking Time: 10 minutes
Servings: 2

Ingredients:

- 2 tomatoes, halved
- 1 Tbsp. fresh basil, chopped
- Olive oil cooking spray
- Salt and black pepper, as required

Directions:

1. Preheat the air fryer to 320°F and grease an air fryer basket.
2. Spray the tomato halves evenly with olive oil cooking spray and season with salt, black pepper and basil.
3. Arrange the tomato halves into the air fryer basket, cut sides up.
4. Cook for about 10 minutes and dish out onto serving plates.

Nutrition:

Calories: 22
Fat: 4.8g
Carbohydrates: 4.8g
Sugar: 3.2g
Protein: 1.1g
Sodium: 84mg

290. Eggplant Bites

Preparation time: 10 minutes
Cooking time: 8 minutes
Servings: 2

Ingredients:

- 1 eggplant, peeled
- ½ tsp. garlic powder
- Cooking spray

Directions:

1. Cut the eggplant into small bites and sprinkle them with garlic powder and cooking spray.
2. Place the eggplants in the air fryer.
3. Cook the vegetables for 8 minutes at 375°F.

Nutrition:

Calories 151
Fat 6.5g
Fiber 8.2g
Carbs 15g
Protein 11.5 g

291. Coated Mushrooms

Preparation time: 10 minutes
Cooking time: 6 minutes
Servings: 2

Ingredients:

- 1 cup mushrooms
- 2 eggs, beaten
- 1/3 cup almond flour
- 1 tsp. sesame oil
- ¼ tsp. dried marjoram

Directions:

1. Mix together almond flour and dried marjoram.
2. Then dip every mushroom in the egg and after this, coat in almond flour.
3. Place the mushrooms in the air fryer in one layer and sprinkle with sesame oil.
4. Cook for 3 minutes on each side at 400°F. The cooked coated mushrooms will have a light brown color.

Nutrition:

Calories 162
Fat 7.7g
Fiber 1.2g
Carbs 14.5g
Protein 9.1 g

292. Oregano Green Beans

Preparation time: 10 minutes
Cooking time: 15 minutes
Servings: 5

Ingredients:

- 8 oz. green beans
- 1 oz. oregano, chopped
- ½ tsp. salt
- 1 Tbsp. coconut oil, melted

Directions:

1. Sprinkle the green beans with salt and oregano.
2. Then brush the green beans with coconut oil gently and place them in the air fryer.
3. Cook the vegetables for 15 minutes at 355°F. Flip green beans after 10 minutes of cooking.

Nutrition:

Calories 283
Fat 21.7g
Fiber 1.5g
Carbs 3.9g
Protein 17.6 g

293. Tofu Potatoes

Preparation time: 10 minutes
Cooking time: 20 minutes
Servings: 1

Ingredients:

- 1 Yukon gold potato
- ½ tsp. avocado oil
- ¼ tsp. salt
- ½ tsp. ground black pepper
- ¼ cup tofu, shredded
- ½ tsp. chives, chopped
- ½ tsp. low-fat sour cream

Directions:

1. Coat Yukon gold potato with avocado oil and sprinkle with salt and ground black pepper.
2. Place it in the air fryer and cook for 20 minutes at 350°F.
3. Then place the cooked and soft potato on the plate and mash it gently.
4. Sprinkle the potato with tofu, chives, and sour cream.

Nutrition:

Calories 125
Fat 10.1g
Fiber 0.4g
Carbs 1.4g
Protein 7.3 g

294. Crunchy Zucchini

Preparation time: 10 minutes
Cooking time: 5 minutes
Servings: 7

Ingredients:

- 3 zucchinis, trimmed
- 1 tsp. chili flakes
- 1 Tbsp. coconut oil, melted
- ½ tsp. salt

Directions:

1. With a spiralizer make spirals from zucchini.
2. Squeeze zucchini spirals a little and dry them with a paper towel.
3. Sprinkle the vegetables with chili flakes, salt, and coconut oil. Shake well and place in the air fryer.
4. Cook zucchini spirals for 5 minutes at 400°F. Shake the vegetables every 2 minutes to avoid burning.

Nutrition:

Calories 30
Fat 2.1g
Fiber 0.9g
Carbs 2.8g
Protein 1 g

295. Salty Baby Potatoes

Preparation time: 5 minutes
Cooking time: 25 minutes
Servings: 4

Ingredients:

- 2 cups baby potatoes
- 1 tsp. salt
- 2 Tbsps. olive oil

Directions:

1. Mix together baby potatoes, salt, and olive oil.
2. Place the vegetables in the air fryer and cook for 25 minutes at 355°F or until the potatoes are golden brown. Shake the vegetables every 5 minutes.

Nutrition:

Calories 146
Fat 8.4g
Fiber 3g
Carbs 16.3g
Protein 2.2 g

296. Onion Pasties

Preparation time: 20 minutes
Cooking time: 4 minutes
Servings: 4

Ingredients:

- 1 onion, diced
- 1 tsp. coconut butter
- ¼ tsp. Italian seasoning
- 5 oz. yeast rolls dough, diabetic-friendly
- 1 egg yolk
- ¼ cup mashed potato
- Cooking spray

Directions:

1. Toss the coconut butter in a pan and melt it. Add onion and Italian seasoning.
2. Cook the onion for 5-6 minutes over medium heat or until the onion is soft.
3. Then mix together onion and mashed potato.
4. Roll out the dough and cut it into 4 rounds.
5. Place the onion mixture on every dough piece and fold it into pasties.
6. Whisk the egg yolk. Brush the pasties with egg yolk and spray with cooking spray.
7. Place the pasties in the air fryer and cook them for 2 minutes from each side at 400°F or until the pasties are golden brown.

Nutrition:

Calories 171
Fat 6.9g
Fiber 2.2g
Carbs 22.7g
Protein 4 g

297. Carrots and Turnips

Preparation Time: 10–20 minutes
Cooking Time: 9 minutes
Servings: 4
Ingredients:

- 2 turnips, peeled and sliced
- 1 small chopped onion
- 1 tsp. lemon juice
- 1 tsp. cumin, ground.
- 3 carrots, sliced
- 1 Tbsp. extra-virgin olive oil
- 1 cup of water
- Salt and black pepper, to taste

Directions:

1. Preheat the air fryer to 350°F and grease an air fryer basket.
2. Mix all the ingredients in a bowl and toss to coat well.
3. Arrange the vegetables in the air fryer basket and cook for about 20 minutes, tossing once in between.
4. Dish out onto serving plates and serve hot.

Nutrition:
Calories: 170
Fat: 9 g
Protein: 1 g
Sugar: 5 g
Carbs: 19 g
Fiber: 7 g
Sodium: 475 mg

298. Instant Brussels Sprouts with Parmesan

Preparation Time: 10–20 minutes
Cooking Time: 3 minutes
Servings: 4
Ingredients:

- 1 lb. Brussels sprouts, washed
- 3 Tbsp. Parmesan, grated
- 1 lemon juice
- 2 Tbsp. butter
- Salt and black pepper, to taste

Directions:

1. Preheat the air fryer to 320°F and grease an air fryer basket.
2. Put the sprouts in your air fryer oven, add butter, pepper, and salt and stir well.
3. Add the lemon juice and stir again.
4. Cook for 15 minutes, turning once during cooking. Add more salt and pepper if necessary, and Parmesan cheese on top and serve.

Nutrition:
Calories: 230
Fat: 10 g
Protein: 8 g
Sugar: 5 g

299. Braised Fennel

Preparation Time: 10–20 minutes
Cooking Time: 14 minutes
Servings: 4
Ingredients:

- 2 fennel bulbs, trimmed and cut into quarters
- 3 Tbsp. of extra-virgin olive oil
- ¼ cup of white wine
- ¼ cup of Parmesan, grated
- ¾ cup of veggie stock
- ½ lemon. juiced
- 1 garlic clove; chopped.
- 1 dried red pepper
- Salt and black pepper, to taste

Directions:

1. Set your air fryer oven on the "Sauté" mode; add the oil and heat it.
2. Add garlic and red pepper, then stir well. Cook for about 2 minutes.
3. Add fennel, stir and brown it for about 8 minutes.
4. Add stock, salt, pepper, wine, and close the lid and cook at high for about 4 minutes.
5. Quickly release the pressure, open the lid, add the lemon juice, more salt and pepper if needed, and cheese.
6. Mix to coat, divide among plates, and serve.

Nutrition:
Calories: 230
Fat: 4 g
Protein: 1 g
Sugar: 3 g

300. Carrot and Oat Balls

Preparation Time: 25 minutes
Cooking Time: 10 minutes
Servings: 3

Ingredients:

- 4 carrots, grated
- 1 cup rolled oats, ground
- 1 Tbsp. butter, room temperature
- 1 Tbsp. chia seeds
- ½ cup scallions, chopped
- 2 cloves garlic, minced
- 2 Tbsps. tomato ketchup
- 1 tsp. cayenne pepper
- ½ tsp. sea salt
- ¼ tsp. ground black pepper
- ½ tsp. ancho chili powder

- ¼ cup fresh bread crumbs

Directions:

1. Start by preheating your Air Fryer to 380°F.
2. In a bowl, mix all ingredients until everything is well incorporated. Shape the batter into bite-sized balls.
3. Cook the balls for 15 minutes, shaking the basket halfway through the cooking time. Bon appétit!

Nutrition:

Calories: 215
Fat: 4.7 g
Carbs. 37.2 g
Protein: 7.5 g
Sugars: 5.6 g

Chapter 10. 30 Day Meal Plan

Day	Breakfast	Lunch	Dinner
1	Air Fryer Hard Boiled Eggs	Beef Korma Curry	Mustard-Crusted Sole
2	Air Fryer Grilled Cheese Sandwiches	Chicken Fried Steak	Almond Crusted Cod with Chips
3	Air Fryer Hot Dogs	Lemon Greek Beef and Vegetables	Honey Lemon Snapper with Fruit
4	Air Fryer Perfect Cinnamon Toast	Country-Style Pork Ribs	Easy Tuna Wraps
5	Air Fryer Monkey Bread	Lemon and Honey Pork Tenderloin	Asian-Inspired Swordfish Steaks
6	Air Fryer Bacon	Dijon Pork Tenderloin	Salmon with Fennel and Carrot
7	Air Fryer Meatballs in Tomato Sauce	Air Fryer Pork Satay	Ranch Tilapia fillets
8	Chicken Fried Spring Rolls	Pork Burgers with Red Cabbage Slaw	Chilean Sea Bass with Green Olive Relish
9	Mushroom and Cheese Frittata	Greek Lamb Pita Pockets	Ginger and Green Onion Fish
10	Cinnamon and Cheese Pancake	Rosemary Lamb Chops	Asian Sesame Cod
11	Low-Carb White Egg and Spinach Frittata	Delicious Meatballs	Lemon Scallops with Asparagus
12	Scallion Sandwich	Low-fat Steak	Fish Tacos
13	Lean Lamb and Turkey Meatballs with Yogurt	Diet Boiled Ribs	Spicy Cajun Shrimp
14	Air Fried Eggs	Meatloaf	Garlic Parmesan Roasted Shrimp
15	Cinnamon Pancake	Beef with Mushrooms	Quick Shrimp Scampi
16	Spinach and Mushrooms Omelet	Warm Chicken and Spinach Salad	Fried Peppers with Sriracha Mayo
17	All Berries Pancakes	Chicken in Tomato Juice	Classic Fried Pickles
18	Cinnamon Overnight Oats	Chicken Wings with Curry	Fried Green Beans with Pecorino Romano
19	Ham and Cheese English Muffin Melt	Chicken Meatballs	Spicy Glazed Carrots
20	Asparagus Omelet	Stuffed Chicken	Corn on the Cob with Herb Butter
21	Pumpkin Pie French Toast	Duo Crisp Chicken Wings	Rainbow Vegetable Fritters
22	Breakfast Cheese Bread Cups	Italian Whole Chicken	Mediterranean Vegetable Skewers
23	Breakfast Cod Nuggets	Chicken Pot Pie	Roasted Veggies with Yogurt-Tahini Sauce
24	Vegetable Egg Pancake	Chicken Casserole	Swiss Cheese and Vegetable Casserole
25	Oriental Omelet	Ranch Chicken Wings	American-Style Brussels Sprout Salad
26	Crispy Breakfast Avocado Fries	Chicken Mac and Cheese	The Best Cauliflower Tater Tots
27	Cheese and Egg Breakfast Sandwich	Broccoli Chicken Casserole	Three-Cheese Stuffed Mushrooms
28	Baked Mini Quiche	Chicken Tikka Kebab	Sweet Corn Fritters with Avocado
29	Peanut Butter and Banana Breakfast Sandwich	Bacon-Wrapped Chicken	Greek-Style Vegetable Bake
30	Eggs and Cocotte on Toast	Creamy Chicken Thighs	Japanese Tempura Bowl

Chapter 11. Conclusion

Diabetic Air-Fryer Cookbook cookware is ideal for diabetic air-fryers as it cooks evenly and quickly so you can enjoy more time to talk and eat with your loved ones. You will be able to stir-fry food and toast bread with Diabetic Air-Fryer Cookbook cookware, all without sacrificing quality or cleanliness. In addition to being durable, Diabetic Air-Fryer Cookbook cookware is nonstick, so you won't have to waste your time spending ages scrubbing your pans after each use. With a reversible stainless-steel handle, you can carry your air fryer in your hands or on your hip for easy one-hand operation.

Worth buying? Yes! Suppose you're looking for an air fryer that cooks food more healthily. In that case, you need to look at a Diabetic Air-Fryer Cookbook air fryer and other products from the Diabetic Air-Fryer Cookbook Company. Diabetic Air-Fryer Cookbook Air Fryers are a great way to cook healthy foods, but it's important to recognize that cooking can be dangerous if you don't know what you're doing. Cooking safely is essential for anyone who is diabetic or tight on time. To make sure your air fryer stays safe, we wrote Diabetic Air Fryer Cookbook to help you learn how to cook safely.

At Diabetic Air-Fryer Cookbook, we understand that our products' quality is just as important as the quality of our service. That is why we stand behind them with a 12-month warranty. Our warranty covers manufacturing defects and defects in materials and quality.

Take the worry out of your diet with this cookbook brought to you by Diabetic Air-Fryer Cookbook. It contains all the recipes you need to make healthy meals for your family. Included are easy-to-follow instructions for preparing healthy meals during a fast or when you have diabetes. You'll also find ideas for using other foods on your Nutrisystem shopping lists like fresh fruits and vegetables.

The Diabetic Air-Fryer Cookbook is a set of recipes designed for people with diabetes who also have hypoglycemia or low blood sugar. The recipes serve as a quick way to reduce your blood sugar level after eating foods that might cause a hypoglycemic reaction. These recipes were created by registered dieticians and diabetes experts who offer fast and simple options that people with diabetes can enjoy.

This cookbook offers solutions for common situations in which your blood glucose level might go too high, too low, or stay too high for too long after you eat. It covers sweet treats, which might cause more rapid reactions than savory dishes. This cookbook offers over 100 recipes related to these situations, including salt and vinegar potato chips, chocolate-covered cherries, dried apricots, banana oatmeal muffins, and more.

This cookbook is dedicated to anyone who has a family member with diabetes. We know how hard it can be to prepare delicious meals, especially in times of stress and busy schedules! That's why we have written this cookbook. We hope our recipes will help you get back to the good cooking you used to do. We want you to be happy with what you prepare and how you feel when you eat it.

If your family member has diabetes, we are sure they will appreciate your advance notice, careful attention, and the thoughtfulness behind the ingredients that go into each recipe. Hopefully, you will find something in this book that your diabetic family member will like or want to try.

Sometimes cooking for someone with diabetes is difficult. You are probably already aware of this — hopefully the instructions in this book are followed precisely so it will help give everyone involved confidence in what they have prepared. This is a good thing — there are some significant results when faithfulness is given regarding every recipe.

Some tips may help prepare fresh foods and dishes for a diabetic person. With a little planning, everyone can be happy with any meal or snack results they prepare.

Measurement Conversion Chart

WEIGHT

½ oz	15 g
1 oz	29 g
2 oz	57 g
3 oz	85 g
4 oz	113 g
5 oz	141 g
6 oz	170 g
8 oz	227 g
10 oz	283 g
12 oz	340 g
14 oz	397 g
1 lb	453 g

PINCH = 1/8 TSP = 1 GRAM

DASH = 1/16 TSP = ½ GRAM

VOLUME

1 tsp	5 ml
1 Tbsp	15 ml
¼ cup	59 ml
1/3 cup	79 ml
½ cup	118 ml
2/3 cup	158 ml
¾ cup	177 ml
7/8 cup	207 ml
1 cup	237 ml
2 cups	473 ml
4 cups	946 ml

Gas Mark	Fahrenheit	Celsius
¼	225°	107°
½	250°	121°
1	275°	135°
2	300°	149°
3	325°	163°
4	350°	177°
5	375°	191°
6	400°	204°
7	425°	218°
8	450°	232°
9	475°	246°

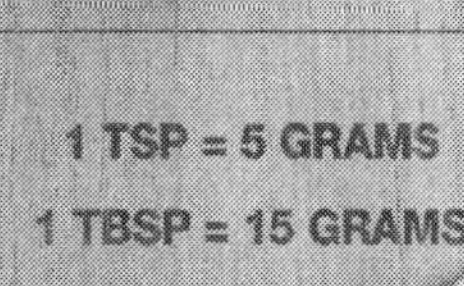

1 TSP = 5 GRAMS

1 TBSP = 15 GRAMS

½ STICK BUTTER = 56 GRAMS

1 STICK BUTTER = 113 GRAMS

Index

Thank you for reading this book

Hello dear reader!
We hope you enjoyed reading this book.
If you did, we would like to ask you to leave a review on Amazon.

In case you were disappointed or if there was something in the book you did not like, please write to us at limelabelpress@gmail.com and share with us your opinion.
Don't forget to include the name of the book you have read.

We value your feedback and always listen to our readers to improve our books.

Thank you for your support!

Made in the USA
Monee, IL
09 October 2024